Landscape Sketching in Pen & Ink

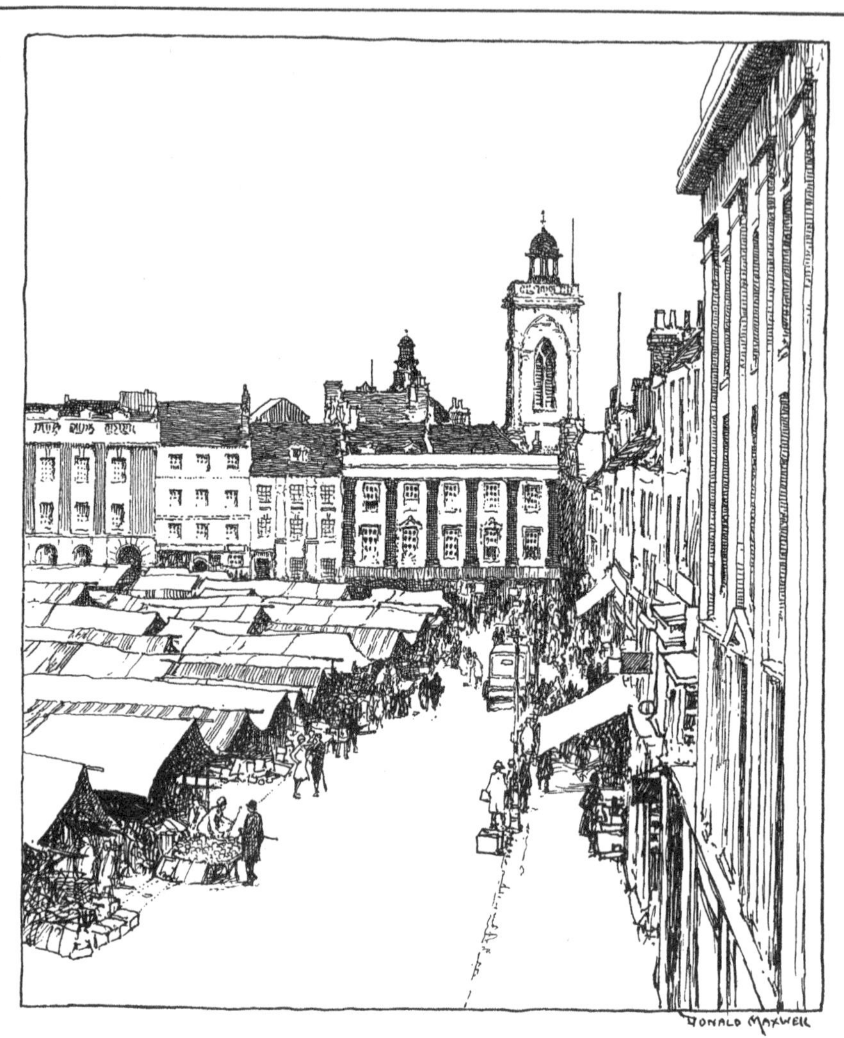

Pen sketch made from a window in the Great Square of Northampton on Market Day

Landscape Sketching in Pen & Ink

With Notes on Architectural Subjects

Donald Maxwell

Foreword by
Gašper Habjanič and Sonja Rozman

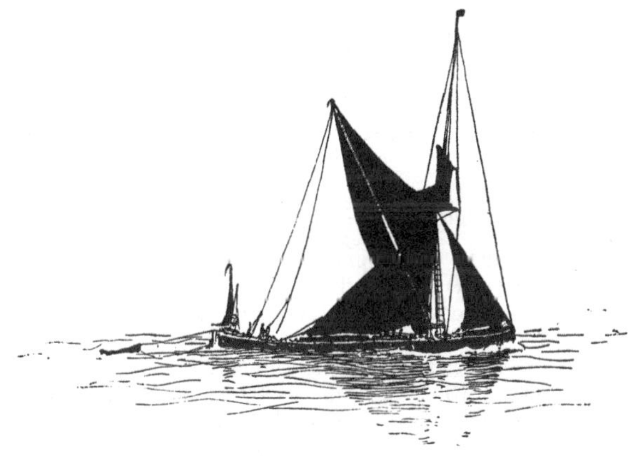

DOVER PUBLICATIONS
Garden City, New York

ACKNOWLEDGMENTS
(Modified from the original edition)

The artist would like to express his thanks to the following artists for allowing him to reproduce examples of their work: Messrs. Frank Brangwyn, Frank Reynolds, and F. L. Griggs.

Also he would like to acknowledge kind permission from publishers and editors as follows: The Editor of the *Church Times*, for use of drawings; Messrs. Anthony Cavendish & Co. 51 Cavendish Road, London, S.W.12, for permission to reproduce various prints that they have published; and the following publishers who have lent drawings from books: Messrs. John Lane & Co., Cassell & Co., Ltd., Macmillan & Co., Ltd., The Faith Press, and the Proprietors of *Punch*.

Copyright

Bibliographical Note

This Dover edition, first published in 2019, is an unabridged republication of the first four parts from *Sketching in Pen and Ink*, published by Sir Isaac Pitman & Sons, Ltd., London, in 1932. For the Dover edition, three illustrations have been retained from Part V (Brangwyn: from "The Book of Bridges," Reynolds: from "Punch," and Griggs: from "Highways and Byways in Sussex"). Twenty-two additional sketches of landscape designs and architecture have been selected for the gallery from the following four volumes:

Chicago Tribune Book of Homes, Chicago Tribune, 1927
Modern Pen Drawings: European and American, The Studio, London, 1901
One Hundred Bungalows, Rogers & Manson, Boston, 1912
Pen Drawing and Pen Draughtsmen, The Macmillan Company, New York, 1920

The Foreword has been specially written for the Dover edition by Gašper Habjanič and Sonja Rozman.

Library of Congress Cataloging-in-Publication Data

Names: Habjanič, Gašper, writer of foreword. | Container of (work): Maxwell, Donald, 1877–1936. Sketching in pen & ink. Selections.
Title: Landscape sketching in pen and ink : with notes on architectural subjects / Donald Maxwell.
Description: Garden City, New York : Dover Publications 2019.
Identifiers: LCCN 2018047986 | ISBN 9780486834283 | ISBN 048683428X
Subjects: LCSH: Landscape drawing—Technique. | Pen drawing—Technique. | Architecture in art.
Classification: LCC NC795 .L36 2019 | DDC 743/.836—dc23
LC record available at https://lccn.loc.gov/2018047986

Printed in Canada
83428X06 2025
www.doverpublications.com

FOREWORD

Drawing in pen and ink is a technique that hasn't changed technically from its beginnings until today. Although its purpose might have shifted from a naturalistic depiction of reality toward expression and recording of the artist's thoughts, the technical process remains the same. Still, taking a book in your hands that was written almost a century ago on the topic of drawing can be revealing and exciting.

Maxwell's *Sketching in Pen and Ink* was first published in 1932. Today one can read it in two ways that reveal two different layers of information. The first is intended by the author at the moment of its publishing—to give advice and present techniques on how to illustrate landscapes in order to tell a story. The other side of the book is most likely unintended by the author, but perhaps even more valued today—it is an insight into the thoughts of a master from a century ago, from the golden era of illustration.

Donald Maxwell was a British illustrator active at the turn of the century. He was a master of storytelling through images in which everyday landscape scenery takes on a lead role in a narrative. Between the challenging motives on one hand and the constraints of the reproduction techniques of his time on the other, Maxwell managed to create stunning imagery that surpasses what one would think is possible with pen and ink. Through his illustrations Maxwell presents places, points to the main characters, sets the emotion, and creates a picture of a whole, coherent story that is still understandable today.

A landscape, the subject of most of Maxwell's drawings, is a very complex concept to depict if one wants to convey a story. It is not only a hard task in visual arts but a general challenge to the human mind. When observing a landscape, our brain instantaneously reduces the number of visual cues it takes in and focuses on the essential. This has been important for us during our evolution.

Being able to focus when scanning a rich and complex environment has enabled us to find food, shelter, and avoid danger. To try to depict such a rich view as a landscape, an artist has to apply the same process our brain uses to scan scenery—abstraction. It is a complex process that Maxwell tackles with full awareness in the book. He compares drawing to talking—you can say a great deal about something, or keep silent.

Maxwell's deep knowledge of the landscape and the natural and human processes that shaped it helped him understand his subject and tell a better story about it. His ability to carefully observe and reinterpret produced amazing imagery that conveys not only structural elements of a landscape but also weather, delicate light conditions, atmosphere, and, most importantly, his thoughts. The results are beautiful images that are not only excellent in composition but also carry the narrative and document information that has kept that additional value a century later.

Maxwell believed everyone can learn to draw. Although not an easy task, he manages to technically explain his results. He demystifies the secret of an artistic creation and plainly and effectively explains it to the reader. His emphasis is on the ability to think and be aware of the meaning and message of each line. He deconstructs and lays his process wide open for the reader to understand. On examples of his drawings, he explains the choice of view, the process of making pencil outlines, the mapping of materials' textures, and finally, rendering in ink. He warns about common mistakes and gives useful tips on techniques of image reproduction from that time, its pitfalls, and how to avoid them.

The technique Maxwell shares with us in his book is a combined result of the need to tell a story through an image and the nature of the tools and printing techniques of the time. The author and his contemporaries had to think about the delicate process their work had to go through in order to be reproduced and published in a newspaper or a book. That had a direct impact on the drawing style and content. Reading about the types of considerations, such as deliberately broken lines or the removal of birds on the horizon that would end up as smudges by the end of the reproduction process, encourages us to consider the publishing techniques we use today in an age of digital reproduction.

Even if we no longer print images in the same manner to reproduce them, the lessons from the book are still relevant, since the technique of drawing in pen and ink has not changed. The true value lies in the descriptions of the images, gathered from Maxwell's earlier books. The author does not only give tips on how to shade, set a composition, or draw vegetation but also explicitly explains the processes and his thoughts behind each image in the book. This is where we learn, for the value is in learning the process, not copying an image. The author's detailed descriptions of his thoughts also give us an exciting and unique opportunity to peek into the mind of a master. We see what ideas and doubts he had and what problems he faced when working on a piece. It reminds us of the questions we ask ourselves today, and we realize that they might be quite similar. This brings us closer to the author and allows us to understand his work better.

Today, drawing in pen and ink does not have the role of the documentation it had in Maxwell's time when it was regularly accompanying text in books and newspapers. It would seem to make little sense to carry a sketchbook around today when a view can be captured through a photograph with devices we carry in our pockets. And yet, sketchbooks, pen, and ink have not disappeared. We can observe a return to the analog, especially travel sketching, where a drawing has taken on a different kind of demonstrable role. It documents the artist's thoughts about a certain place in a certain moment. What is the story of that moment? Which part will I tell, which part will I leave out, and which part will I invent new? These are the questions Maxwell essentially teaches us to ask ourselves.

GAŠPER HABJANIČ
SONJA ROZMAN
November 2018

PREFACE

I HAVE so often been asked why I have not written a book on sketching in pen and ink, that when Sir Isaac Pitman & Sons suggested the same thing for their technical library I felt bound to do so without delay.

I must make some sort of apology inasmuch as I have illustrated these essays entirely from my own sketch-books. This would appear to be vanity. It is, however, really a kind of special modesty.

It would be an impertinence for me to attempt to tell you how such masters of line as E. J. Sullivan or F. L. Griggs interpret nature, but it is likely that I shall be able to speak with some helpfulness on technical problems which I myself have solved. I will not say that these problems have been solved always with complete artistic success, but with *some* success nevertheless.

I am writing chiefly for those who are going to get their living by illustration or who are about to try their skill in the arena of public competition. Therefore, I will not hesitate to point out—to encourage the others—that all the sketches published in this book have been in one direction a success. They have not blushed unseen or wasted any such sweetness which may be theirs upon the desert air. Editors of newspapers and publishers of books have at least parted with money for them—and that is *something.*

At least it can be said of the author of this book that he did not take as his motto: "Do as I say and not as I do." I cannot tell you without fear of contradiction the best way to draw. The thing is highly controversial. I can tell you, however, *one* way to draw, and when you have mastered that way wish you all good luck in finding others.

DONALD MAXWELL

CONTENTS

PART I

THE PROBLEM OF SKETCHING WITH PEN AND INK

The pen is the one instrument of drawing in the use of which no instruction is needed. Any one who can write a postcard or put down a column of figures is perfectly well equipped technically to make a sketch in line.

Let us, therefore, start straight away and draw something without any further argument or any suspicion of what psychologists name the inferiority complex.

We will draw a brick.

Anybody can draw a brick.

On page 4, in the right hand bottom corner, is an outline of a brick marked *B*. It you don't like this brick go and find a better one. Take a foot rule and measure it. You will ascertain that it measures, as viewed in a wall, 8½ in. by 2½ in.

On page 5, this same outline, marked *B*, is filled in with a series of downward strokes. A line along the bottom will bind these together and a line at the end, a little thicker than the others, will denote that the brick goes no farther to the right. In fact, these bottom and end lines show the brick as lighted from the top left corner of the paper.

You will say, I know, that it is all very well drawing a brick, but what about perspective and art and technique and poetry—hang it all a man can't draw a picture if he hasn't got a gift.

You are quite right in some ways, but you do not argue that it is silly to attempt to write an account of a football match unless you can be Shakespeare, nor futile to be able to multiply by six if you are not Einstein.

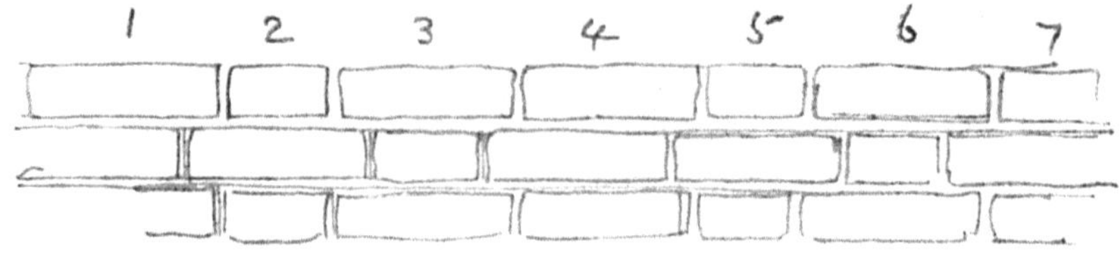

FIG. 1
Bricks in a wall drawn in outline

In the Middle Ages most people of culture, the highest in the land, had to send for a priest if they wanted to write their names or read a simple message sent in writing from a neighbouring manor. King John, as a matter of cold fact, never signed Magna Carta, for all the assertions of the history books. He could not write his name, so he made a mark like a squashed frog and the Archbishop of Canterbury wrote it in for him.

This all seems very ridiculous to us, but it is not more ridiculous than the system of culture under which we live in the Merrie England of to-day, when we have to send for an artist if we want to draw a brick.

Now we have learnt to draw a brick for ourselves. And if we can draw a brick we can draw many bricks: we can draw a wall, a gate, a tower. In fact, we can draw, with due patience and a plumb line, anything that a man has made. If a man, not highly skilled as the fine arts go, can put brick on brick and thus build a wall, so can any one with a pen and a piece of paper put brick on brick and make a representation of a wall.

Here is a piece of wall. In Fig. 1 the bricks are drawn in pencil outline. In Fig. 2 that same piece of wall is shown in pen and ink. The various shapes have been filled in and the pencil lines rubbed out. Now note the different character in the bricks and the method of toning with lines to show that character. No. 1 is a new brick, a smooth plane of bright red. The general appearance of this brick in black and white is well expressed by the careful, almost parallel and firm lines that shade it. Brick No. 3, however, is an old one. It must be expressed with a less orderly and less parallel set of lines and these will give it a rough and battered appearance. Note that the mortar has come out and the join between this brick and the

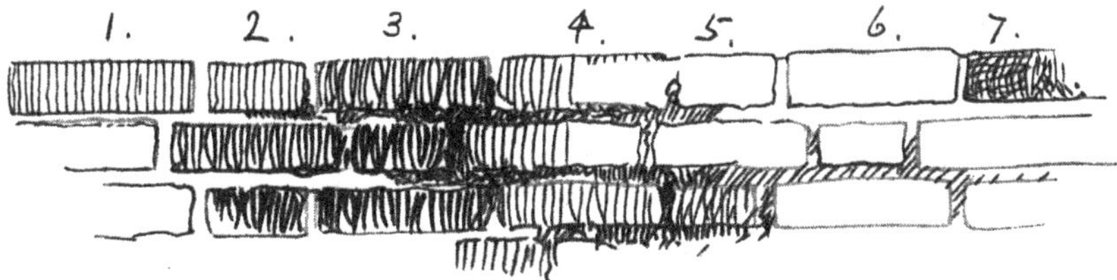

Fig. 2
Bricks in a wall toned to represent varying colour and age

brick below it is hollowed out and therefore in shadow and expressible by black marks.

At bricks 5 and 6, however, and the zone underneath them, there is a zone that has been whitewashed, though now rather dirty and going grey in the mortar between the bricks. Thus the simple outlining of the bricks and the slight toning with a few fine lines of the mortar, will give the appearance of a lime-washed wall or one made of very light coloured bricks.

If you will come with me only a few steps outside my studio, we will make a study of an old and rather tumble-down part of my house, a subject a little more advanced than this strip of brickwork. It is a bit of the Tudor fragment left when the house was rebuilt in the time of Queen Anne. In fact, it has at this date, I think, been rebuilt to some extent itself. The red bricks are not part of the original work, which would all have been in stone. It is the old bake-oven of the farmhouse, and the fact that it is in very bad repair is all the better for our purpose.

There is plenty of time, so we will fetch a chair and sit down to the job. A distance of about ten yards will suffice for scale, and we will avoid any perspective problems by taking up our position at right angles to the wall. We will measure each bit carefully. Let us begin by a definite statement that is well within our powers so far as we have advanced at present. Let us draw one brick as we did at *B*. We, therefore, set down our brick at *X*. In the pencil sketch in Fig. 3 we will mark this brick with an *N* to remind us when we come to detail and expression that it is a new brick and it must be shown as such if we are to express our piece of wall effectively.

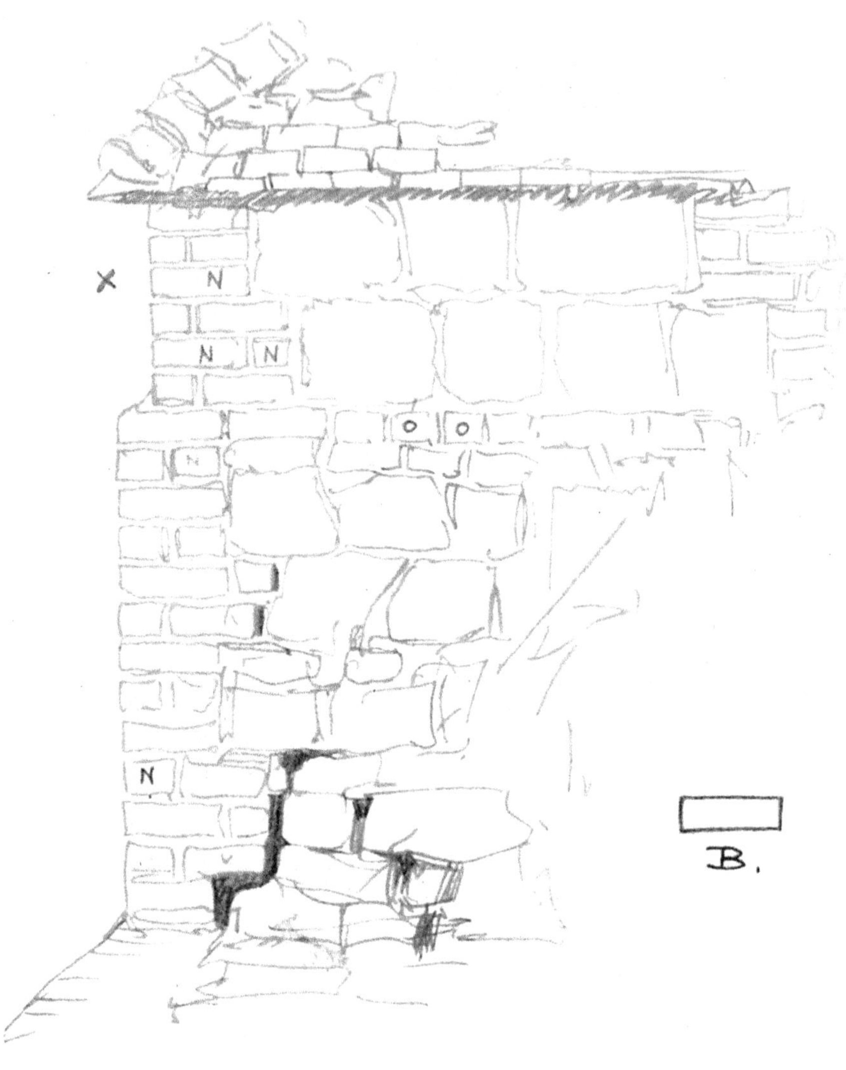

FIG. 3
Pencil sketch of a piece of wall

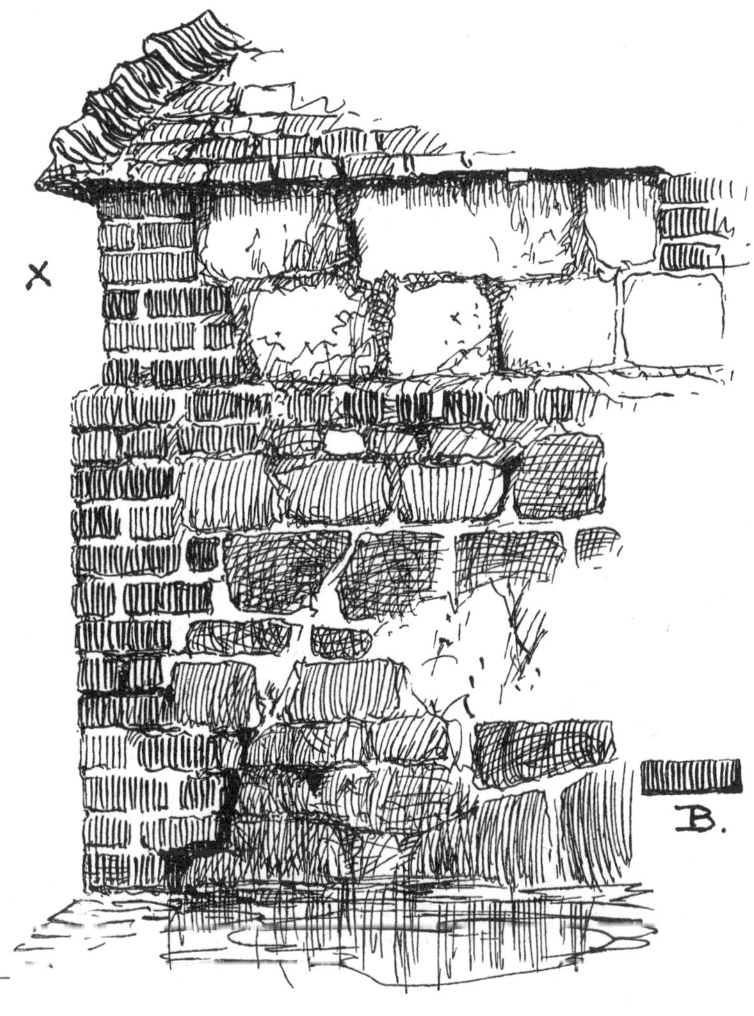

FIG. 4
The same sketch carried on in pen and ink and the pencil work rubbed out

Then let us show the two bricks above it and the one just under the tiles. Then we will outline the two bricks below our brick *N*, and still farther below that, two more bricks, which are newer than most of the work. These we will also mark *N* to remind us.

Before we go any farther, let us get down this much in ink. Brick *X* we can shade with careful and evenly distributed straight vertical lines and we will treat the other two new bricks in the same way. Then we will put in the two bricks under *X* with rougher and darker lines, and so, brick for brick, expressing old or new, dark or light, until we have this little section of brickwork well nigh complete. From this definite and accurate statement we can add on and measure out other parts.

In the brick course, underneath the stonework, are two outlined bricks in Fig. 3, each marked *O*. This reminds us that they are old. They are darker and more crumbled than some. It is a good idea to put these letters *N* and *O* on different features in a wall because we may take your pencil sketch home and finish the pen work at leisure. Weather and other circumstances will often stop us being long before a subject, but an accurate pencil outline thus lettered will stand us in good stead.

Then, as in Fig. 3, we will complete our outline of the principal shapes of the various component parts of our wall, not forgetting to indicate in deep black those fissures in the masonry that give shadows.

When we come to tone this work and complete our statements about it, we shall have to devise some method of "colouring" the stones—some method of lining that will give them greyness and darkness without making them look like the bricks in surface. The seven large stones in the two top courses are almost white in comparison with the dark bricks. A jagged line here and there and a few dots will break up the surface enough to show their character.

The stones lower down are darker in tone and at the foot of the wall they are considerably stained and toned with moss. We will shade them very irregularly with loose lines to some extent expressing the irregular surface of stone as opposed to the more compact surface of the bricks.

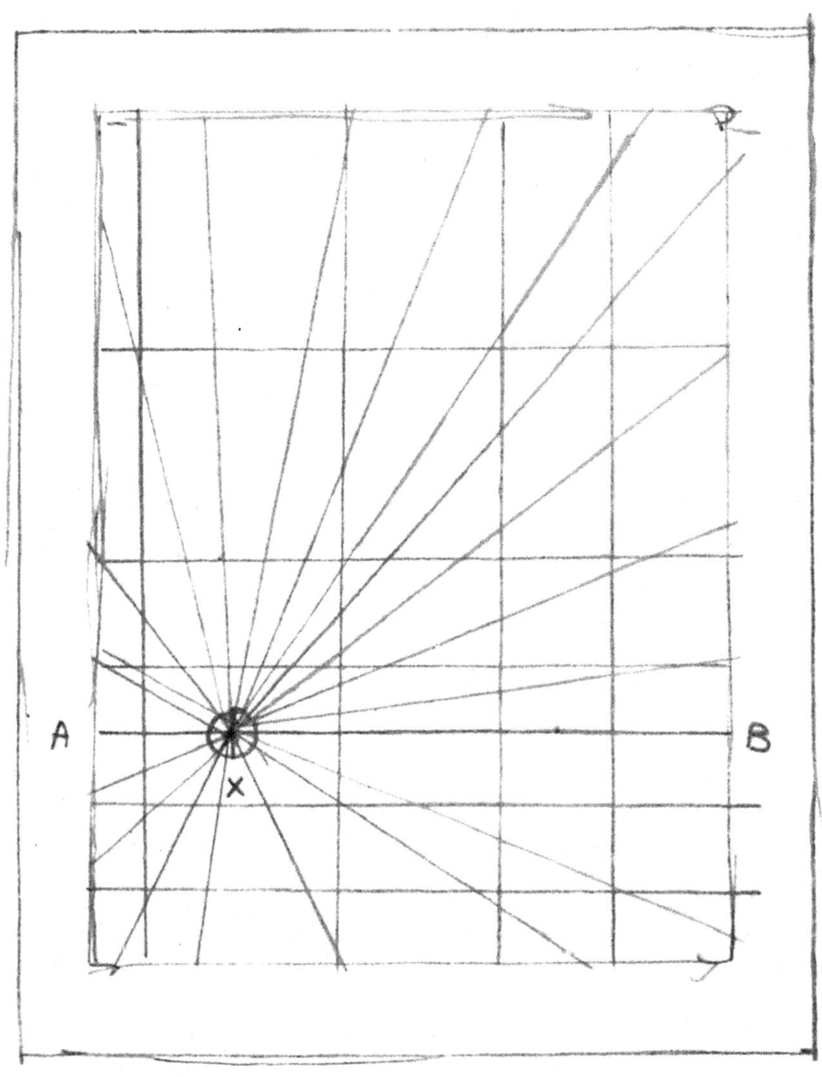

FIG. 5

A pencil skeleton rectangle useful as a check on lines that are horizontal or vertical or "vanishing" in perspective. This pencil work can be rubbed out when the sketch is completed in ink.

It is unnecessary to labour the points mentioned here as it will appear by now that the representation of a complicated mass of masonry with all its fissures and weather stains is really quite easy to draw in pen and ink, although at first sight it looked very difficult.

It will not be possible, however, to find views in which a wall is so conveniently placed. There will be times when a great deal of a building is seen in perspective, and this, again, at first sight seeming far more complicated than it really is, means mastering fresh problems. I have often found it very useful to have a few sheets of my sketch-book ruled out in pencil as in Fig. 5, on page 7. The outer line here represents the edge of the page in the sketch-book. The line *A–B* is the position of the horizon. *X* is the vanishing point.

In choosing a view, take care that the vanishing point is in the picture. In a street scene, for instance, it would be well to find a position on the left-hand side of the road (assuming that the most interesting part of your projected sketch is to be the right-hand side of the street with its buildings.

As a rough rule you might say (in spite of certain exceptions caused by uneven ground) all horizontal lines in the architecture of walls fronting the street wherever they come—the tops of windows and doors, steps, pavement, parapets—will be on the radiating lines that converge to *X*. All horizontal lines of buildings and walls at right angles to the road will be on lines parallel to *A–B*, and all vertical lines will be parallel to the sides of the frame.

In Fig. 6 we have a very quickly drawn—it is almost scribble—view of the side of a castle and beyond it a square tower. Because it is placed on this pencil framework as seen in Fig. 5—rough as it is—we are certain of a few facts about it.

I have purposely drawn the sketch Fig. 7 very badly, but in spite of that fact, it can be seen that there is a castle here, and beyond it a square tower. It would be possible to build up on this and put in more and more detail as in Fig. 4. Such few lines as were in the original pencil scribble and in the beginning of the pen drawing as seen in Fig. 7 are right as far as they go.

With these diagrams, Figs. 6 and 7, it will be well to expound a method of securing the right position for figures and objects in a view. How often do we see pictures with boats and people in them. The boats are sinking or dancing up in the air, and the people in the distance are too big and in the foreground too small.

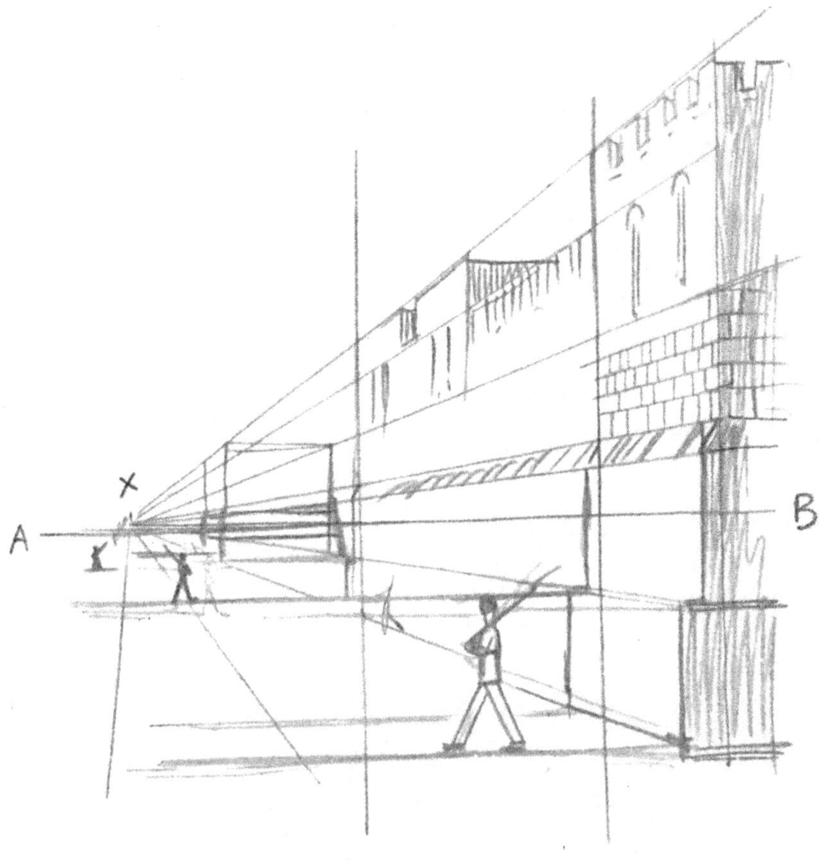

FIG. 6

A quick pencil note made on such a framework as that shown in Fig. 5

A good analysis of the problem of placing things is this. The horizon, wherever the sketcher should be, is on the level of his eye. If he is standing up by a boy four feet in height and by a post twelve feet high, and in various parts of the picture are four-foot-high boys and twelve-foot-high posts, the horizon will be always over the heads of the various boys and the posts will always overtop the horizon, wherever they are, by the same proportion of their height.

In the case of the tin soldiers in Figs. 6 and 7, you will note

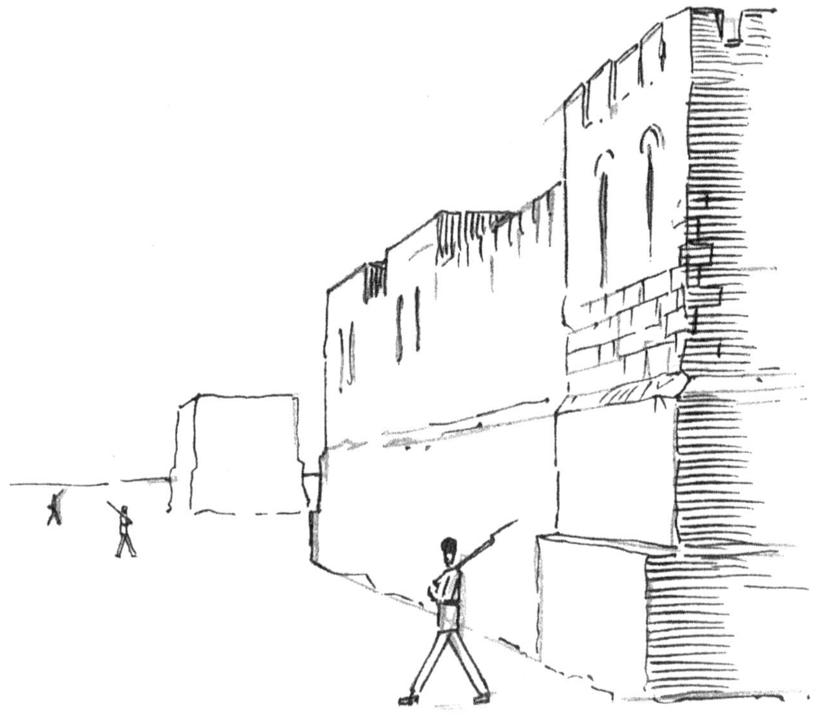

FIG. 7

Certain features of this rough sketch, however unsatisfactory they may be in some ways, are "right" in perspective.

that the head of the soldier comes always half his height below the horizon. Crude as these diagrams are—they are meant to be crude—you will note that these tin soldiers, wherever they are marching, are in correct position for the distance at which they are supposed to be.

Fig. 8

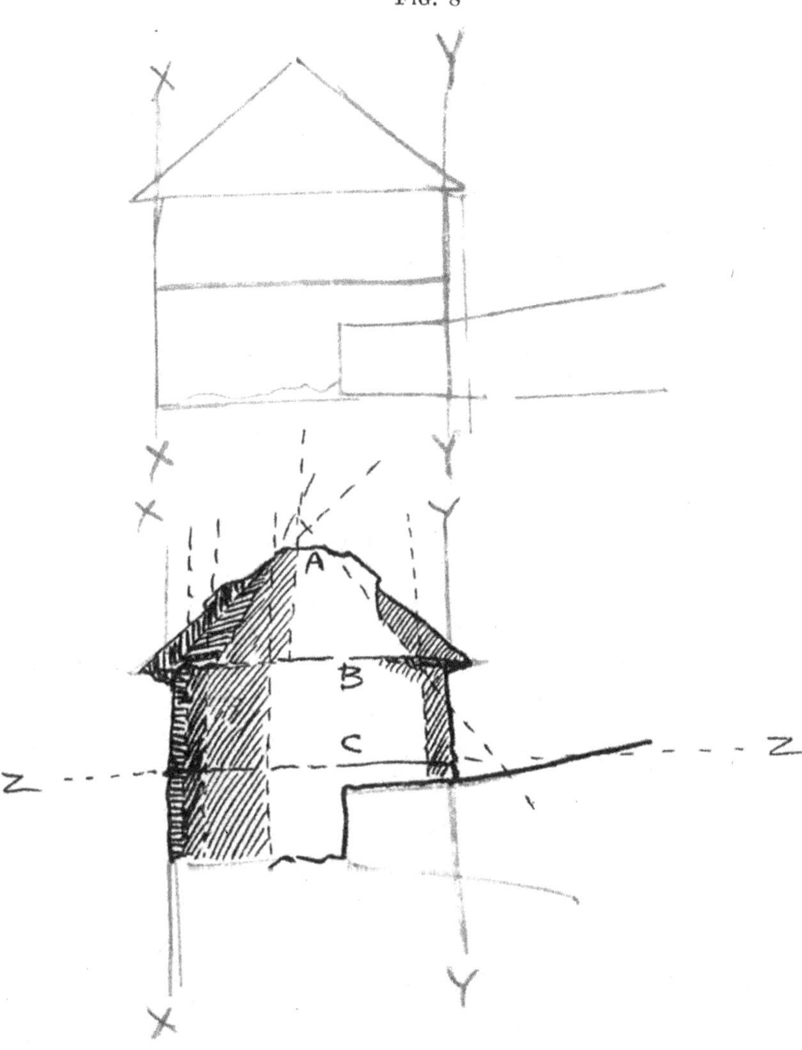

Fig. 9

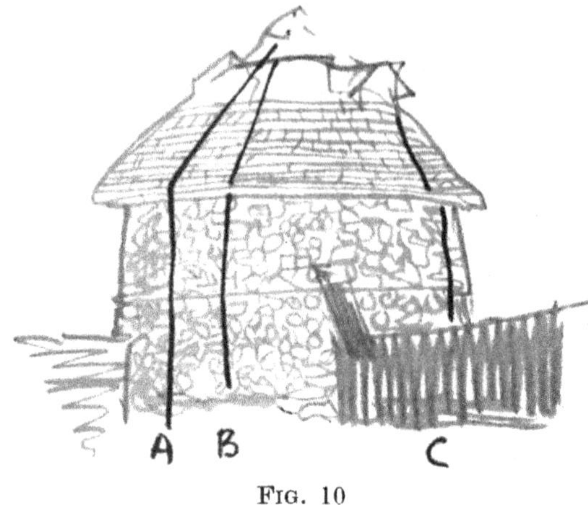

FIG. 10

Now let us take a subject that is a little more ambitious. We will walk down the road and draw the old dovecote. It is shown opposite. For purposes of instruction, we must for the moment imagine that this drawing is the actual thing. We are now to set ourselves the problem of representing it with lines. The level marked **Z–Z**, in **Fig.** 9, is the height of the eye of the sketcher. Thus, although the dovecote is round, there is no curved perspective line to worry us here. This course in the masonry (which conveniently coincides with the horizon) can be represented with a straight line.

Let us take the diameter, as it appears at arm's length, and mark it off by the straight vertical lines *X* and *Y*. This is near enough at present, although the sides of the tower are not straight. Then we will measure the height of the roof and put it in as in Fig. 8, with two straight lines and a bottom line which is straight.

As in Fig. 9, however, we must "correct" on this rough outline. We are looking *up* at the roof, so the line we have made straight (at bottom edge of roof) must curve. It will be nearly straight in the middle and drop a little at each end—in fact, this curve must be part of an ellipse. Also, the sides of the building must be made to bulge.

We must apply the same methods in sketching this dovecote as we employed before in sketching the old wall, but there are difficulties here of a new kind. The wall was flat and this is round. How are we to *show* that it is round?

In Fig. 10 we have made a rough sketch of the "facts" of the dovecote. This is a first putting down of the joins between stones and tiles and the outlines of things in general. It is obvious,

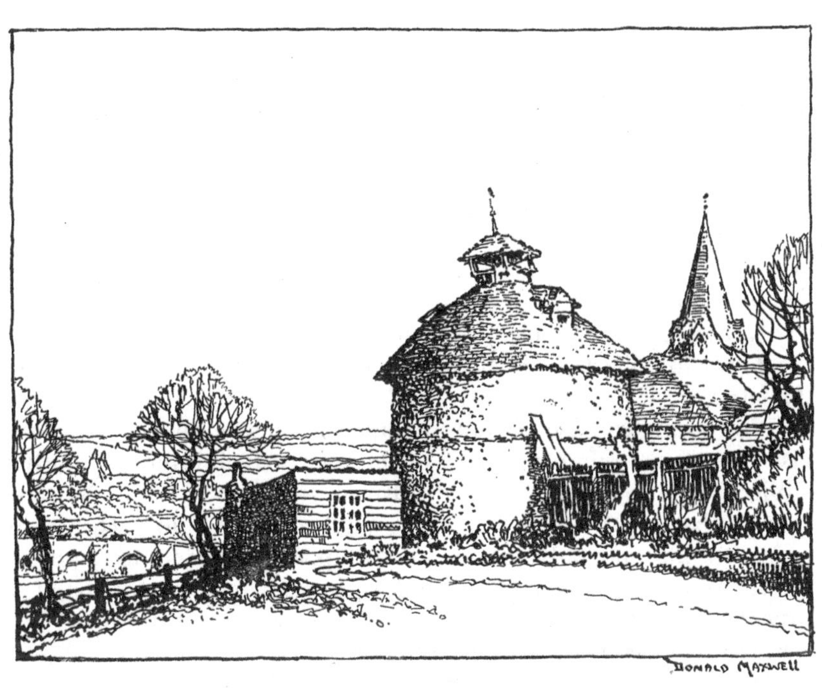

THE OLD DOVECOTE, EAST FARLEIGH

(Cavendish)

however, that the building does not appear to be round. There is not enough emphasis of light and shade.

Now, in Fig. 9 the different zones of light and shade are shown. The full light is along the zone *A–B–C*, and as we get round to the left, which is the shadow side, our tone must get darker and darker. In Fig. 9, too, we have put in shading lines which give some idea of the roundness. They are purposely put in "unintelligently," i.e. although we can see now that the dovecote is round, the shading lines do not tell us anything else about it. However, by making our shading *also* represent the marks of tiles or stones *as well as degrees of shadow* we can, as in sketch on page 13, approach to some better likeness of the thing represented.

We cannot afford to say much about the tiles and stones on the zone *A–B–C* because any elaborate system of lines will give us too much tone. A few dots, but nothing *untrue*, will have to suffice. We must put in more and more detail as we get into the shadows so that our lines are *doing two things*—

1. Expressing nature of the material.

2. Giving light and shade to show the shape of the object depicted.

Now that we have acquired some experience with these exercises, let us use what we know in the way of technique on another subject—the old abbey ruin on page 17—which gives a problem that we have not tackled before. What are we to do with a very uninteresting and ugly garage mixed up with a romantic ruin.

It cannot be left out because if we leave it out we shall have to invent something in its place, and in the present state of our experience we shall not be able to do this.

Here is the answer. Drawing is like talking. You can talk a great deal about a thing or you can be silent. In this case, of the garage, *we will say very little about it,* but we will not make any statement that is not true. With skilful handling, the very plainness of the shed may be made to act as a foil to the richer details of stone walls and tiled roof with which it is contrasted.

Let us use this subject as a means of testing the value of what we have learned in our previous drawings. First, we will draw a plain but accurate outline of the main objects in the view (Fig. 11). Then we will take note of different surfaces and different "material"

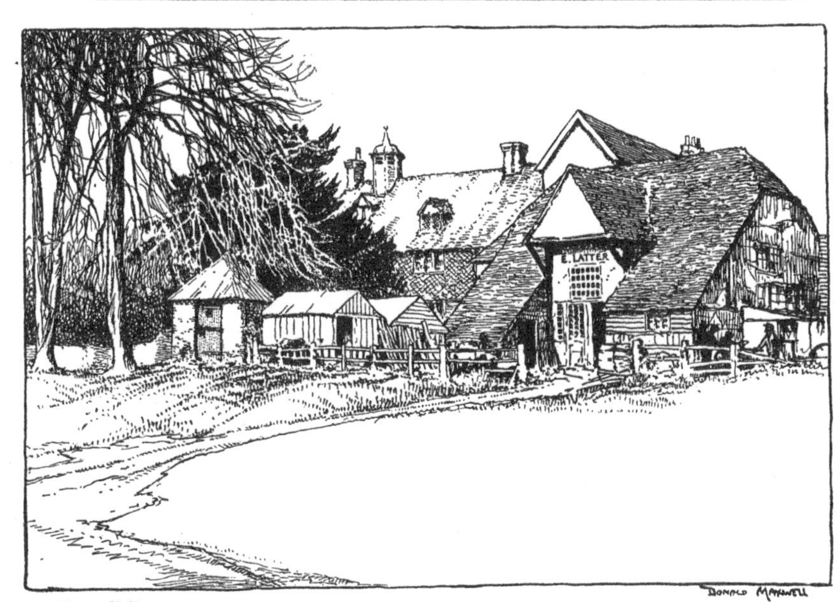

(*Cavendish*)

YALDING

A sketch made to show the importance of leaving out unnecessary detail where the sense of lightness is to be maintained

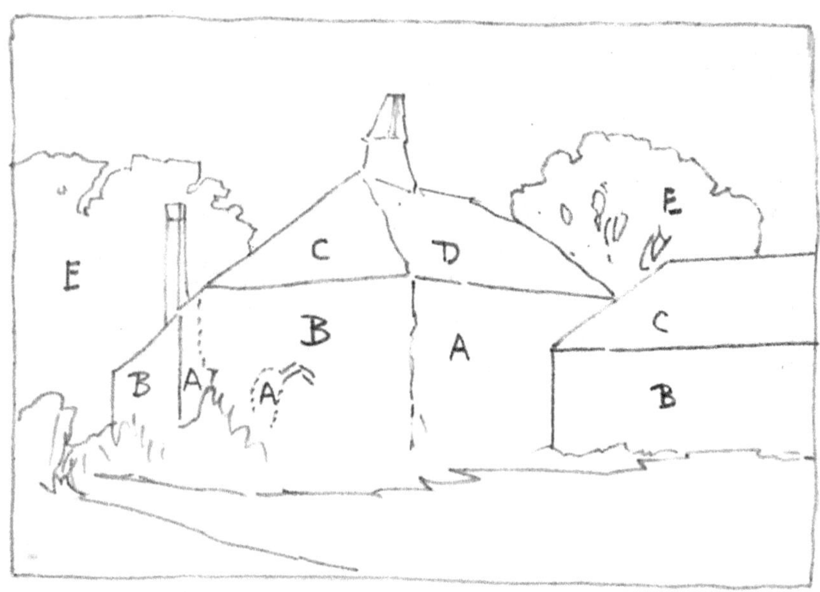

FIG. 11
Pencil outline and diagram of principal features of sketch opposite

within those outlines. All the walls that are in shadow we will mark *A*. The sunlit walls we will mark *B*. Roofs facing the sun we will mark *C*, and this roof in shadow, *D*. *E* represents trees.

Make a careful "map" of the masses of foliage and then fill it in with any texture (as we found useful in "Headcorn Mill") that will be broken and open and expressing a tangle of parts. The sunlit surfaces marked *B* we will draw as we drew the old wall, and the shadow surfaces *A* we will put in with an open crossed line. The garage, however, we will indicate with a firmer and straighter line because it is new. Of the roof of the garage we will say nothing—we will leave it blank, and there must be an economy of detail in the lighted part of the old roof, but more linear work on the shadow side. The little sketch of Yalding on page 15 is another example of this method of treatment.

When the shadow of a large building is seen at some distance there is probably little or no detail visible within it. By this

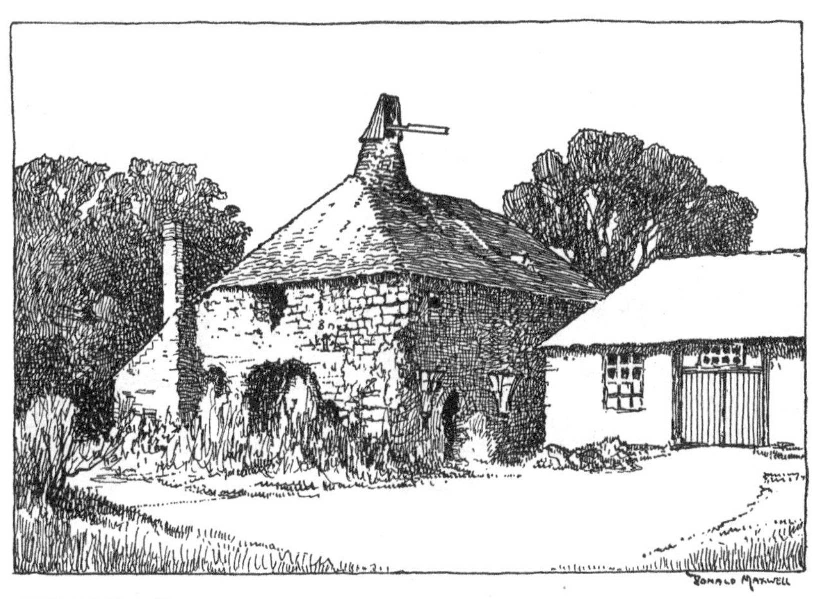

("*Church Times*")

FRAGMENT OF AN ABBEY AT ROBERTSBRIDGE

absence of detail, the idea of distance is often conveyed. On page 18 we have fragments of the drawing of Winchester. They are reproduced the same size as the original work. Perhaps these will give hints to those experimenting with various problems of representation.

I have purposely said nothing about pens or paper used, because in starting out I argued that the veriest beginner has nothing to learn in the way of equipment. I assume that you are using the same pen with which you would write a letter, and similar paper.

However, now that we are getting more ambitious and going farther afield for subjects a few notes may be of use. Do not use a paper that is rough. A smooth cream or white paper that will take quick strokes without "kicking up" will suffice. People will often tell beginners to work on Bristol board, smooth and dead white. Personally, I hate any very hard white surface. It stares

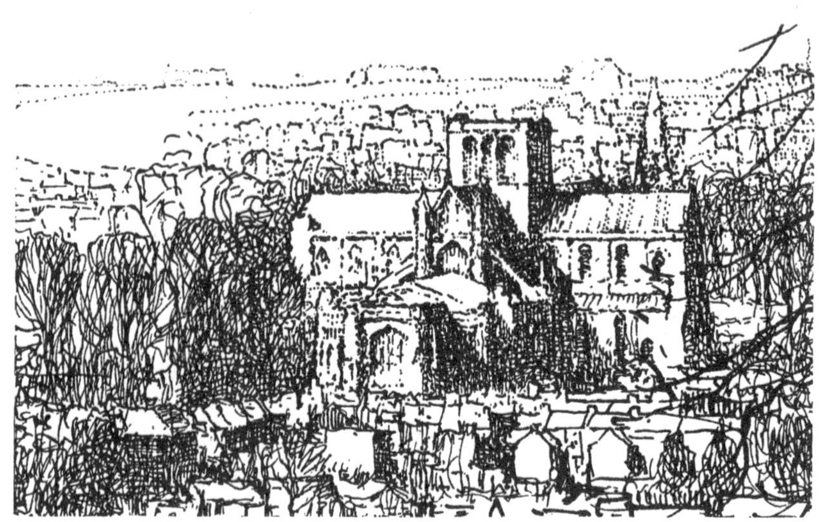

Fig. 12

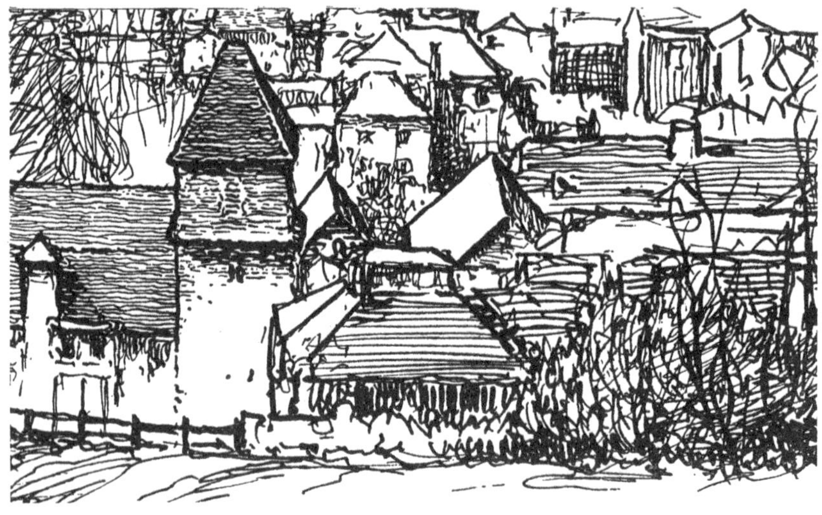

Fig. 13

Fragments of the Winchester sketch on opposite page, reproduced exactly the same size as in original work

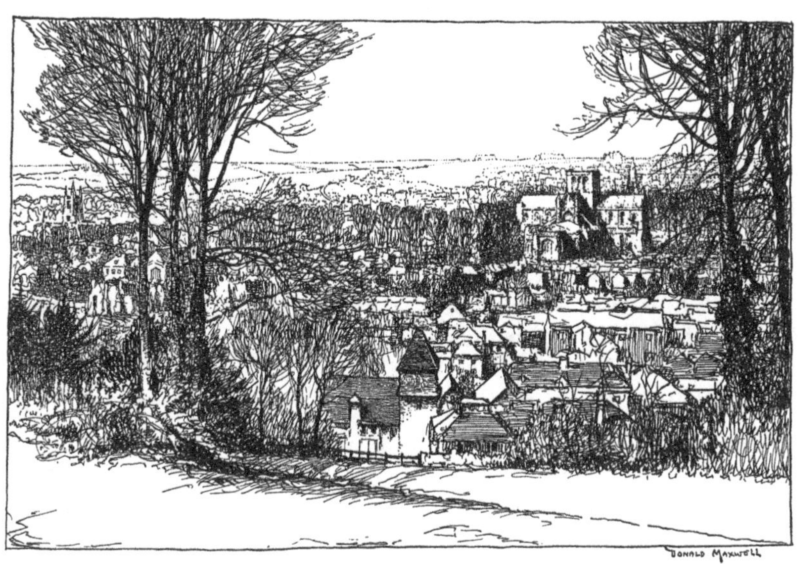

(Cavendish)

WINCHESTER

The sketch of Winchester reproduced above is from an original about 17 in. in diameter. It is reduced in size far more than desirable, but owing to this open nature of the pen work its details stand this reduction fairly well. On the page opposite are two fragments from this drawing, and they are reproduced in facsimile. The comparison is instructive, and shows the nature of the modification that reduction in size renders.

the artist out of countenance. Any paper that is not very strongly grey or deep yellow will reproduce effectively at the engravers.

As to pens, when you gain confidence and speed you may find a necessity for a pen a little more "fluid" and pliable than the one with which you are accustomed to write.

I, myself, am doing these with a moderately fine Waterman fountain pen. The choice of nib should be a matter of experiment. Any good maker of fountain pens will help you in choosing, and many will go so far as to lend you one for experiment. The nuisance of carrying ink about, to say nothing of spilling it, is a strong argument for a fountain pen. A great deal of time is saved, too, with a fountain pen, and there are many "jet black" inks to be had. Avoid any sort of purple ink as you would avoid the Evil One. If you make a false stroke leave it until you get home. Work over it and then, with a razor blade or with a touch of Chinese white, obliterate your mistake.

Well, now you have made a good start. In the next chapter you will become a professional.

PART II

PROBLEMS OF TECHNIQUE IN PEN LINE AND THE PLANNING OF A PICTURE

We can now assume that we have to some extent mastered the art of representing the things that we see. We can make outlines to show their shape. We can fill in these outlines in such a way that the lines we put down reveal the nature of the substance represented—brick, stone, wooden palings, tiled roofs, woodwork, etc. We have learned to make such lines of representation that we can show the difference between trees and walls, between grass and flagged wall, and between masts of ships and bare winter trees, quite apart from their shapes. And now we want to go farther, become more ambitious, and make our efforts worthy of being regarded as pictures.

"It is all very well," said a pupil to me, "to sit down and draw a wheelbarrow or an object in view, but I get completely baffled with the choice of a picture. I don't know where to leave off and where to put the four boundaries of my work."

Many other artists, artists who are by no means beginners, are often baffled by this problem. It is necessary to have some sort of rule as to what is your picture-frame in this view. Each one must fix this for himself.

I think a good limit, one I use roughly myself, is to include in your composition all that is covered by your sketch-book held in front of you at arm's length and no more. Thus, everything you see comes within the compass of what you can measure and check easily in starting your work. I am assuming, however, that your book or block is of decent size—say, 16 in. by 10 in.

It is a good plan to think out your composition slightly smaller than this size of the paper. Rule a rectangle 14 in. by 8 in., thus leaving one inch all round. Let this margin appear as a mount. You will then learn to build up your drawing on a definite shape.

Also it gives you a liberal margin of error, for we all make mistakes, and if some important object is edging out of the picture the matter can be rectified by moving the margin which we have been cautious enough to rule in pencil.

We will take a fairly simple subject and a very interesting and picturesque one, so we will go to Aylesford and draw the old bridge. Not a very simple subject, you say, yet the easiest things to manage in pen and ink are often those that appear complicated. For one thing there are plenty of points to measure. The more difficult subject is one of a rolling skyline of gentle undulation. In this there is very little that can be measured with ease and it is difficult when it goes wrong to see quite what is the matter. Not so with this bridge: each arch and each buttress can be checked and catalogued and put in its place.

Let me suggest a method of attack. It is a good idea to have a cut out mount or small frame to hold up and fix in your mind the exact boundaries of your view. Then put in a pencil line to show the horizon—in this case it is about an inch and a quarter from the bottom of picture. Now find the top of the parapet over the big arch which is 1½ in. from the bottom and 2 in. from the left-hand side. From this point measure off the depth to the top of the arch and put in the two buttresses on each side. Since we are making an exact drawing of this scene, without any licence, we can put in this bit completely and finish it in ink. The water is still. We can measure off the reflection. Then measure off the next buttress to the right and put in the arch and its reflection. This is not difficult. So at last the bridge is quite finished.

Having now put the bridge down—and, of course, quite correctly—we have definite points from which we can measure. If we measure upwards from the top of third buttress from the central arch we find the parapet at one inch and a quarter. Thus, with no more art than that required to make a good map we can get outlined all the principal features of the scene.

In a drawing of this kind with a good deal in it, there is no possibility of doing much with small details within the outlines of different objects. In the bridge you will see the markings of stonework and also in the church tower, but you must resist the temptation to put these in your drawing or the surfaces of these

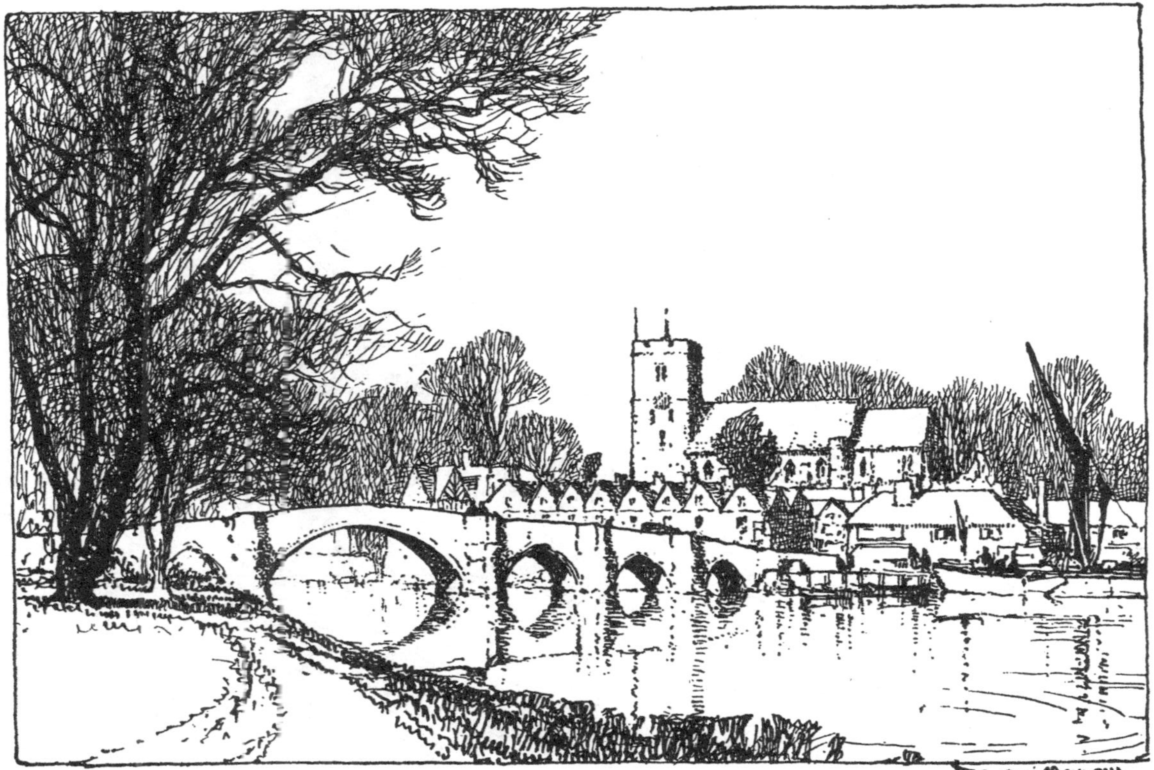

(Cavendish)

AYLESFORD

things will become too dark. The difference between a hard slate roof, as in the next drawing, and a piece of crumbling brickwork can be to some extent expressed by means of the outline.

In the subject "The Bridge at Good Easter," I hope you can guess that the bridge is built of brick and that the roof of the cottage is slate. If you cannot it does not matter—mine is the blame; but take note of the principle and make a practice of outlining objects in such a way that the outline by its nature tells something of the material. The trees, for instance, can be expressed with a broken and dotted line for the boundary of masses of foliage and in the case of the water in the stream, a difficult thing to draw well, it can be expressed by leaving blank paper within a very carefully drawn outline and in this blank space putting a few touches showing reflections. There is no doubt, I think, which is the road and which is the stream, yet by an economy of line one is expressed entirely by its edge and the other by a few touches that anybody could do.

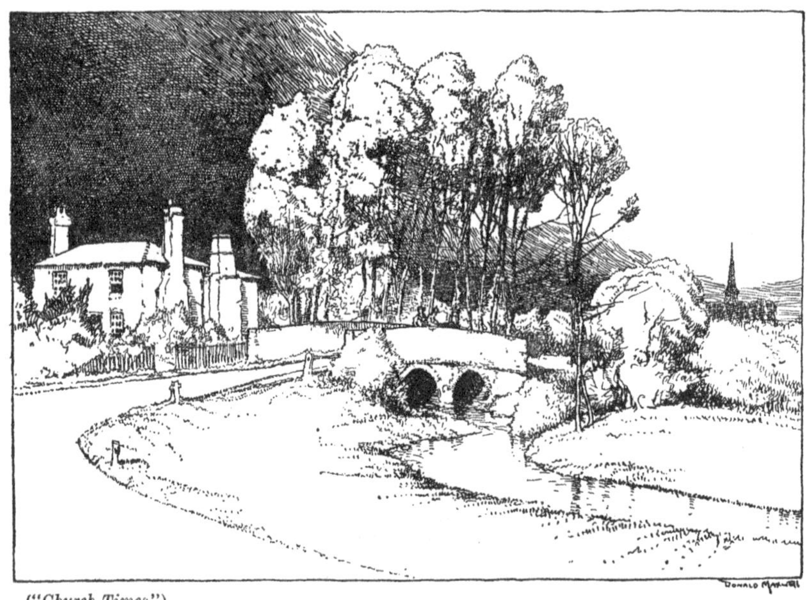

("Church Times")

THE BRIDGE AT GOOD EASTER

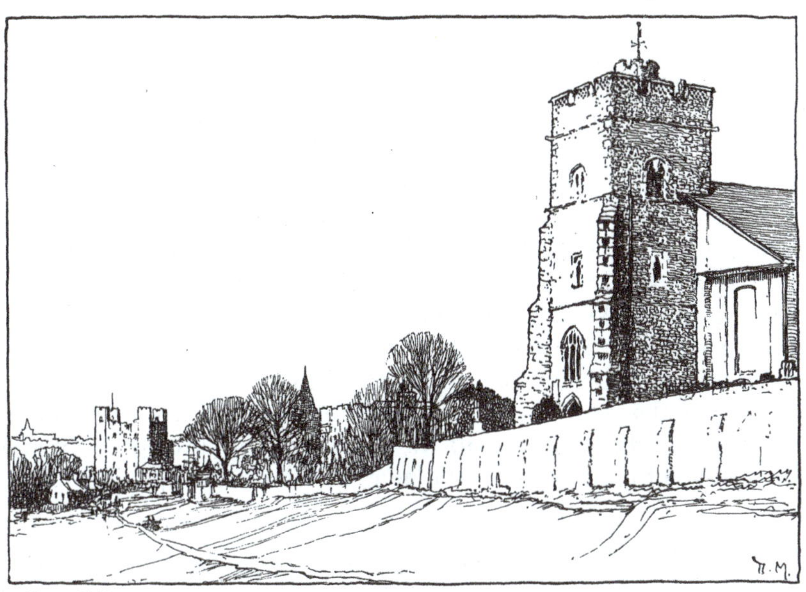

(*Cavendish*)

St. Margaret's and the Castle, Rochester

The sketch of St. Margaret's Church, Rochester, is one that I had to make for a newspaper during the Rochester Pageant. One of the scenes, St. Augustine meeting the Priests of Wodin outside the city, is an incident that took place on a slope by the Medway, almost exactly at the spot where stands St. Margaret's Church to-day. The path across the fields towards the castle is more or less the track of the old road into Rochester. Here is a case where the whole merit of the drawing is in the composition. The Tower of St. Margaret's can be placed on the extreme right. We won't bother about the nave—it is very ugly. We can just get in the castle on the left and by an eighth of an inch within the margin include Frindsbury Church across the Medway, and we have the history of the place in a nutshell. The central spire showing through the trees is the cathedral.

Now for further exercise in "getting things down" in sketching and the device of expressing things by omission let us attack two subjects of somewhat similar feeling—both bits of old Kent. The buildings in these drawings are very much the same in their treatment. The great difference to be expressed is the nature of the ground. One has a foreground which is a farmyard. The other is a corner, well known to motorists, around which they come often, I fear, at a speed that is not always expressive of caution.

The nature of a farmyard is as different as possible from a motor road as anything could be. So in the case of the former a few ragged strokes expressive of straw and mud will be sufficient. Almost any broken lines or dots will keep the eye from travelling over a surface rapidly. Not so the corner of the smooth road. By putting nothing whatever in the way of marks on the main surface of the road and by emphasizing carefully the curves and lines of the edge of the road the eye travels uninterruptedly and the feeling of motion—potential motion, for no car is passing at the

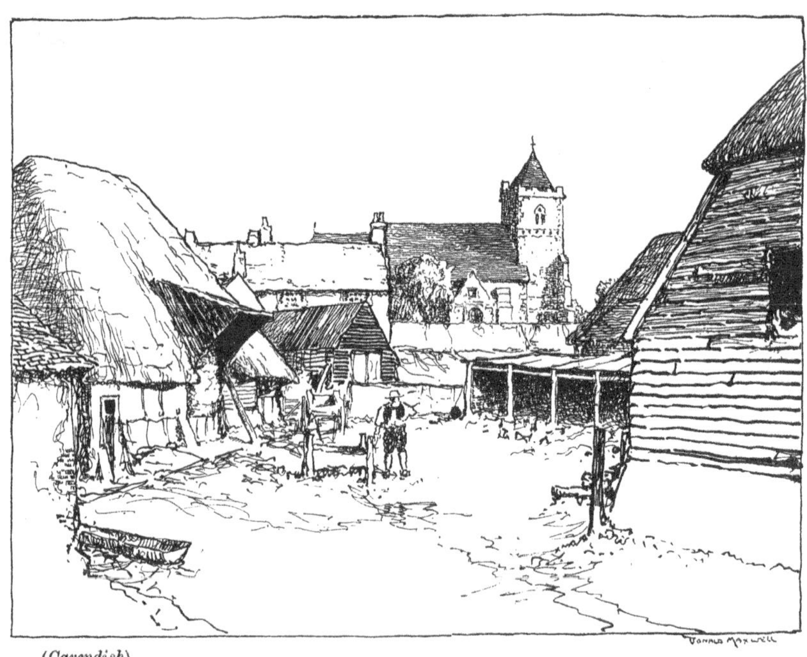

(*Cavendish*)

A FARMYARD IN KENT

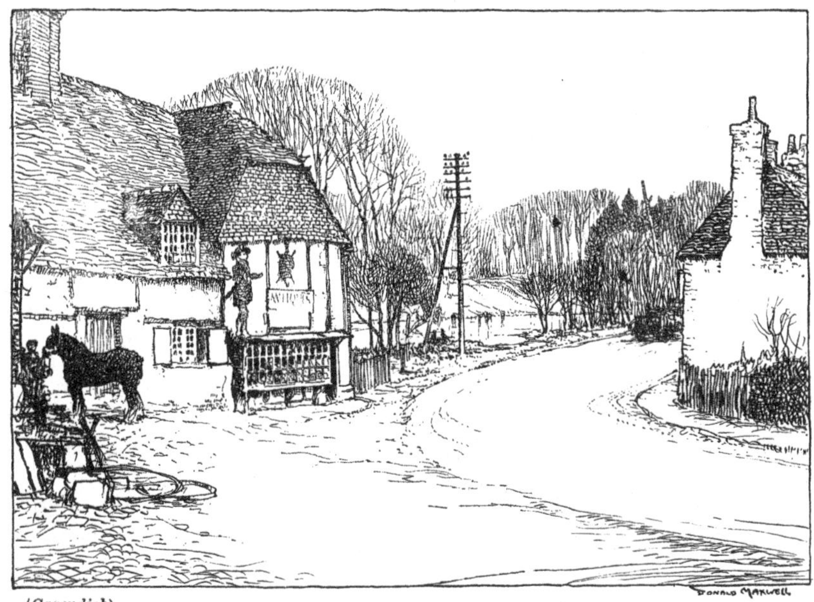

(*Cavendish*)

BLACKSMITH'S CORNER, WESTERHAM

moment—is given to the picture. Beyond the road is a stream, here broadened out to a pleasant sheet of shallow water. The portion of paper on which it is to be presented, however, is about one inch long and only one eighth of an inch deep, and even this small area is crossed by trunks of trees and a telegraph post.

There will not be much room for detail, that is, to show that this surface is water and nothing else. What is to be done about it? The answer is that only one thing can be done that will be successful on this tiny scale. The distant bank must be drawn carefully, and from this some dark points must reflect. A black dot with a series of little black lines in diminishing importance underneath these will suffice. I think, or at least I hope, that it is clear there is some water beyond the road.

I should like to suggest to students who are using this book as a means of building up a technique of their own in sketching, that they should not necessarily adopt the method which I have found useful. There are many ways of drawing, and my method in these different cases is only one.

It would be helpful if a student chose some subject exactly akin to each subject here given as an example, and when he comes to the particular problem of expression mentioned let him try and evolve a pen line or texture that he feels will be eloquent. If it succeeds, well and good; if not, he can begin again and fall back on the device I have used.

Let us study another quite different landscape, in this case a scene in the heart of Dorset. The general shape of almost everything in sight is suggestive of woolly bears. Now if we are not very careful a landscape completely made up of woolly bears of slightly different tones and in slightly differently arranged masses will be rather a muddle. Remember there is no colour at our command, so we must be more than ever careful of our form.

We must think out a treatment that will get some order into our landscape. If we can find a position which will give us some tree trunks cutting across these flocks of woolly bears we shall obtain contrast, something straight to counteract so many curves.

The best expedient that I can think of to get order out of this difficult subject is that of keeping to white paper as the expression of each field or expanse of grass in between the trees or wooded sections. Any attempt to show the different tones of different crops would be fatal, because, however careful we are and however skilful, we shall probably be unable to distinguish spaces of grass from trees. By keeping all our detail for the trees themselves and the group of cottages we show in effect that these are *things* upon the ground, and by delicate copying of the shapes we see we can give the undulation of the country very effectively.

When we come to the cottages, although they are thatched and thus share the blunt outlines of everything else to some extent, we can find some hard, straight lines about them which must be emphasized.

And now from this landscape of gentle curves and undulating surfaces let us take one that gives us a chance of more vigorous expression and more "exciting" adventure. So good-bye to Dorset. We will climb to the savage ridges of Helvellyn and try

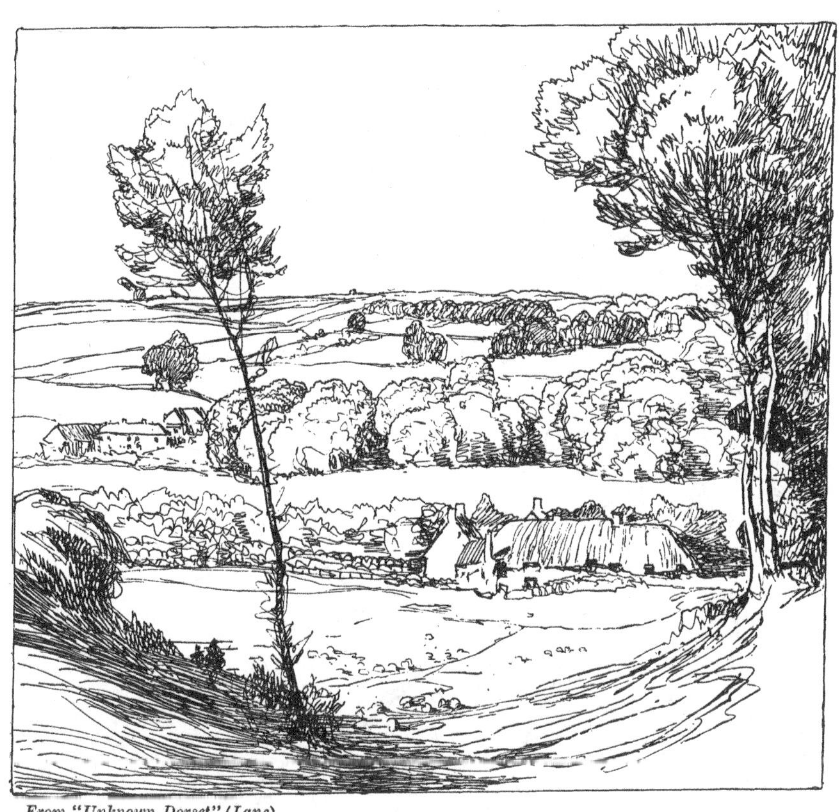

From "Unknown Dorset" (Lane)

THE VALLEY OF DELIGHT

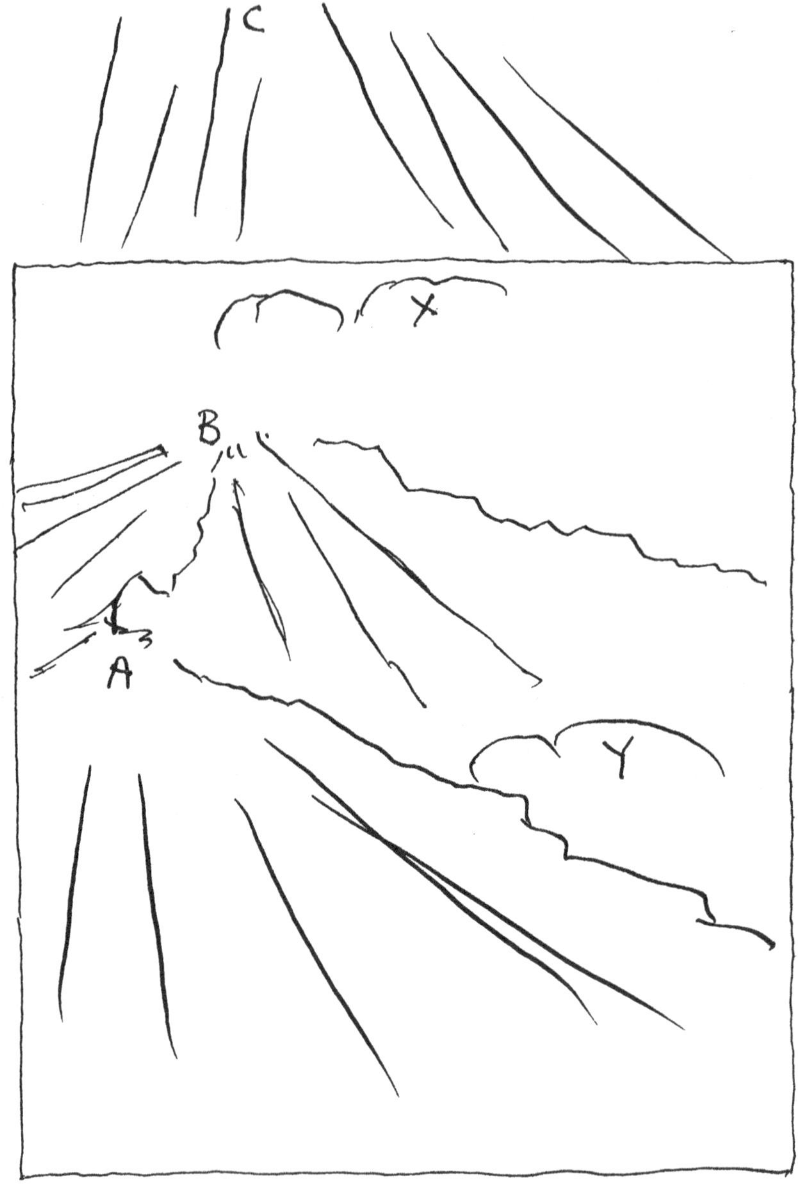

FIG. 14

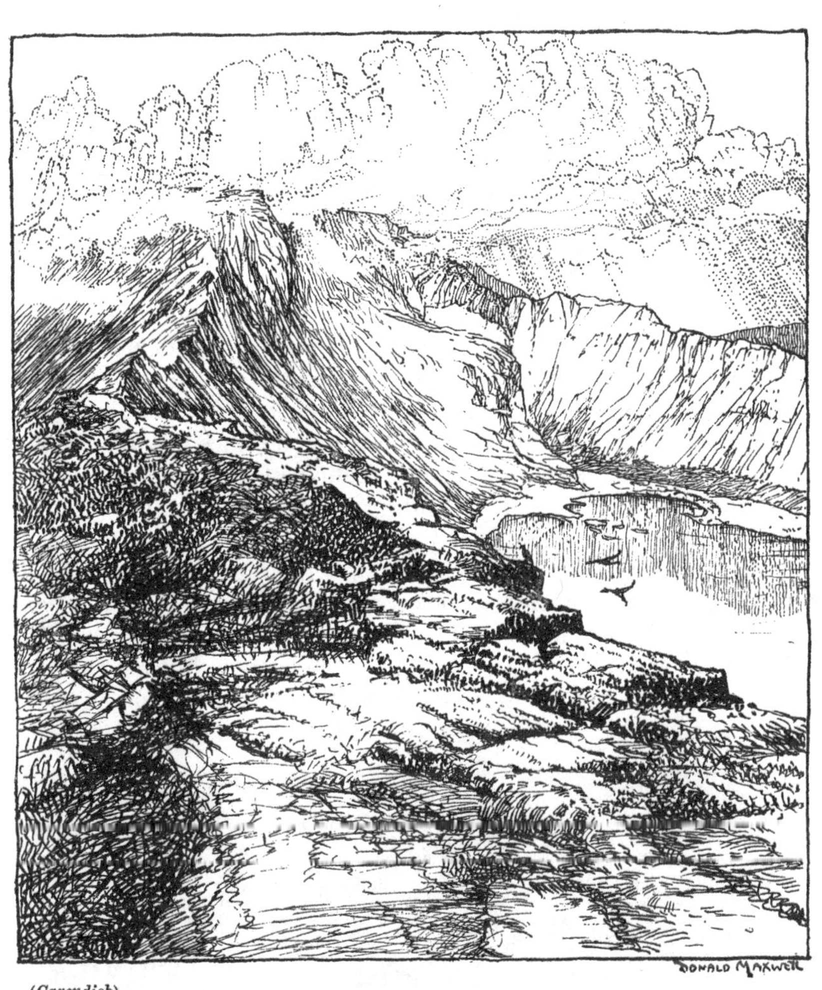

(*Cavendish*)

HELVELLYN

and catch something of the mountain wildness of this romantic lake district.

Now a subject like this is really far easier to draw because the component lines are definitely there. You can actually see lines in these rocks and ridges, whereas in the case of smooth fields or feathery masses of trees you must look for lines or invent them to express the tendency of things and their arrangement.

In this mountain landscape the great sequence of lines that dominate the composition are those that lead to and from the long ridge that reaches the summit in the clouds. Another ridge leads to this from the right, on the other side of the tarn. The point of view chosen is from a ledge of rock on this ridge and in order to maintain a connection with it we must emphasize all lines that lead up towards the peak. I do not mean we should put in anything that we do not see. There are hundreds of lines and ridges and cracks and marks, but, by dwelling on those that converge toward this peak and by dwelling less on the lines and marks that do not, we can succeed in getting a feeling of continuity and show that the track we are on is leading us up to the summit of the mountain.

The diagram, Fig. 14 (on page 30), will show the main lines of the design. There is first a convergence of lines to *A*, then a convergence to *B*, and finally a convergence toward the sun, which is somewhere above *C*. The repetition of the curved lines of the farm by the curved lines of the clouds helps the "eloquence" of the

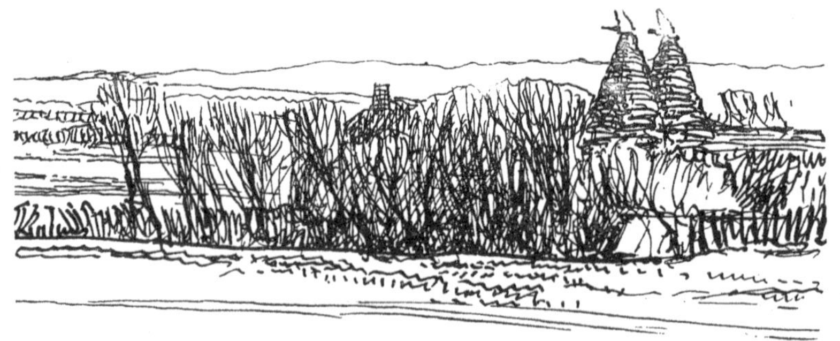

Fragment of sketch, Headcorn Mill, reproduced the same size as original pen work

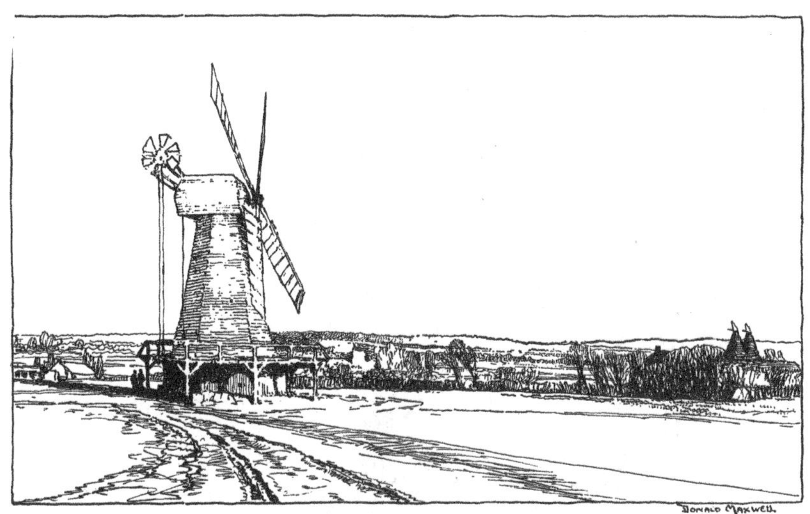

(*Cavendish*)

HEADCORN MILL

design—for these two zones of curved lines are the only parts of the picture not angular and hard. By expressing cloud and water as essentially different from the mountain, we have enormously strengthened the savage feeling of the scene which we want to convey.

As a contrast to this grim mountain picture we will find one of breezy expanse in the Weald of Kent. It is the old white windmill of Headcorn. To get the feeling of wind sweeping across the wold we will stand the mill well on the left of the picture, facing the wind, which is blowing from our right. Of course, the windmill, if it is working, will always face the wind, but think what an uncomfortable picture we should have if the mill were turned round, as it stands here within the margins of the picture, with the wind blowing from the left. The open space in front of the sails seems to express the direction from which the wind is coming, quite apart from the position of the windmill's sails.

I think it will be instructive at this stage for the student to study the sketch of Headcorn Mill above, and then having seen the result of the reproduction, turn to some fragments of its

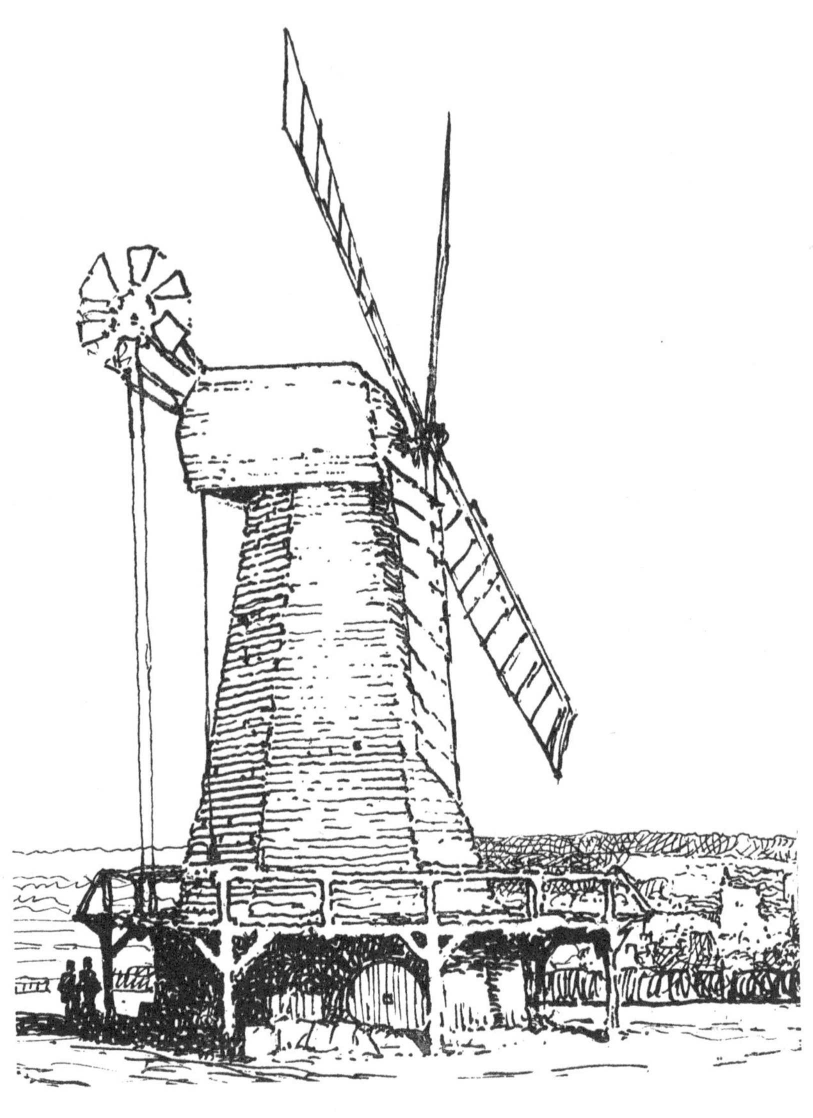

A fragment of the sketch of Headcorn Mill on page 33, reproduced same size as the original pen work

component parts on pages 32 and 34. These bits are reproduced exactly the same size as the original pen work. By comparing this large-scale work with the small-scale reproduction it is possible to see what happens in the way of alteration on account of the great reduction.

The great lesson it is necessary to learn is that pen work in shadows must be kept open. If it is closed in too much, although it may look well in the original drawing it will most certainly fill up and look poor in reproduction on a small scale.

You will note that the rough and very wild looking pen work in the shadows of the trees on page 32 is only scribble within a certain zone. The shape of the trees is very carefully drawn and the scribble is left to take care of itself, *but within well defined boundaries.* The result is that there there are flicks of white of all sorts and sizes gleaming out of the dark tone. These being irregular will not make a noticeable pattern as would a coarse screen, although they are large, and just because these white flicks are large they will not fill up.

At the same time it will be well to note the details in the mill as seen in the original size drawing opposite. The different faces of the woodwork, seen in different degrees of light according to the angle, are toned by nothing but details. The shadow side is made up of lines, but these lines show the planking. On the sunny side many details have to be left out to give light and so the shape is rendered, and the point of this technique is that not one dot or one line is meaningless. Nothing is so depressing as a pen drawing in which the shadows look like some curious kind of coco-nut matting run to seed.

Not all problems of composition can be solved at once. Sometimes they are almost solved by accident. In a sketch I was making in Essex I drew the subject you see on the next page but without the clouds. The day was fine and the light was good and I drew the two mills and the bridge as you see them there, with a little bit of placid reflection in the river.

There was something unsatisfactory about it. The composition looked "silly." The two mills seemed too much alike. Soon, however, some big white clouds came sailing by and I decided to put in a dome of cloud. The improvement in the arrangement of the picture was instant. The flowing line of the clouds seemed to balance the two mills.

On looking at it since, I am convinced, although I did not notice this at the time, that the satisfaction caused by the line of the cloud is that it echoes the general arrangement of the arches of the bridge. This repetition of things, as in the clouds and tarn of the Helvellyn picture, is often a strengthening and satisfying factor in a design. Needless to say the device is one that must be kept in hand. It is like a dangerous drug which must never become a beverage.

Many novices find it very difficult to "do" trees except in their winter aspect. A distant mass of trees seen in the confusion of distance and sunshine is not one of the easiest things to represent. I think I can help some artist, however, by this suggestion. When you find a great wooded slope, as in the Surrey landscape sketched near Leith Hill, do not begin by thinking it is difficult. In this case I sat down and drew each tree as I saw it, a clean line outline of its shape without light and shade. By the time some hundreds of these outlines had accumulated the wooded hill in the sketch

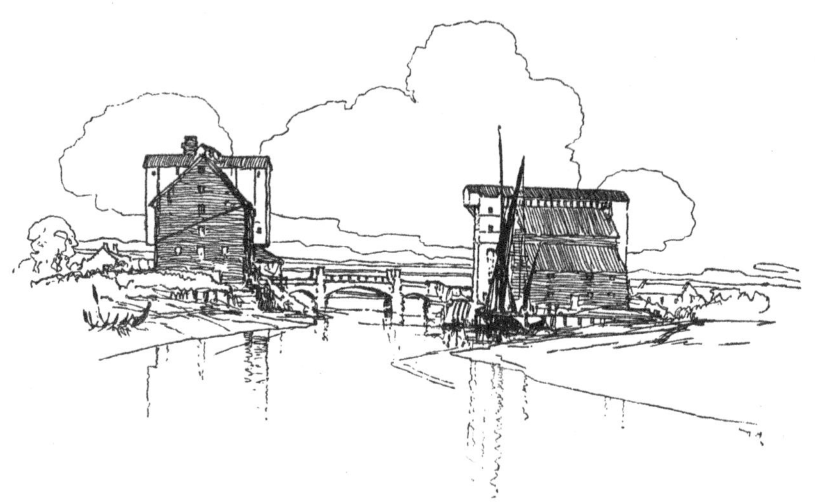

From "Unknown Essex" (Lane)

BATTLEBRIDGE, ESSEX

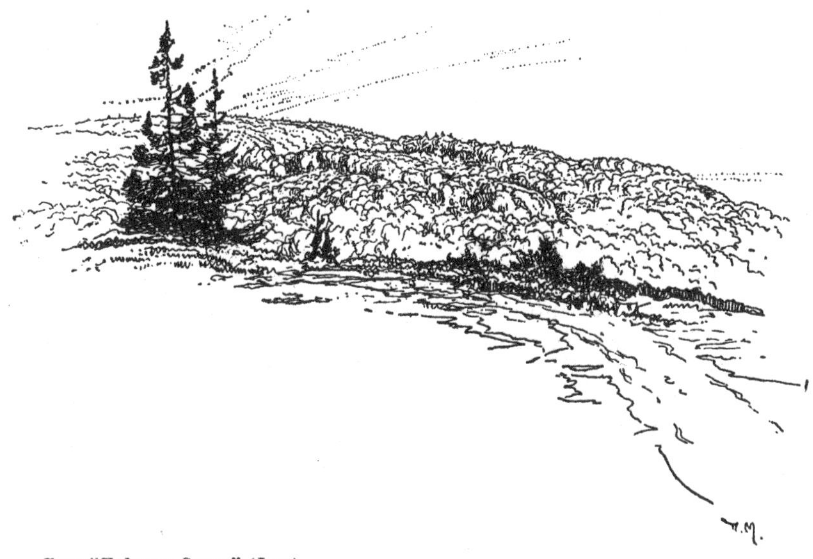

From "Unknown Surrey" (Lane)

NEAR LEITH HILL

(as it should do) began to look very like a distant forest. Then a few cast shadows added and a few omissions, as on the right hand part of the distant ridge, and there is some irregularity of effect as of light and shade playing over the landscape.

Such a vague, but not unpleasing, distance, however, must be seen with something in contrast, or it will be "over sweet." The two black fir trees with their straight stems and angular blocks of foliage are just sufficient to do this.

On this subject of composition and design, it does not in the least matter whether you can analyse a good effect. The little sketch of Cuckfield Church on page 39 was one that I made because it was the most striking view that I saw as I walked about the place.

I can see now, although I certainly did not notice it at the time, that the arrangement of the roof and walls of the workshop of the monumental mason almost exactly echo the shape of the church spire. There is a steep peak and then a splayed out base and, below it, straight walls.

The lines of the houses mimic this, but not so exactly as to be noticeable. The chimney stacks echo to some extent the full shape of the spire and at their base the roofs flatten out as in the base of the shingled spire. Even the tombstones leaning against the wall in two different directions echo the arrangement of the spire.

All this, as I said before, is "unconscious composition." I merely saw a view that I liked and drew it. I am now only trying to explain in technical terms why I liked it.

Another important thing that the beginner should note is the effect of bright sunshine on things. How often do we see a sketch that is evidently intended to give the effect of sunshine which does not look bright.

In the case of a window painted white, as in the workshop in the foreground of this picture, the effect of sunlight is to exaggerate the size of the woodwork and to diminish the apparent size of the panes. Thus by very great enlargement of the white and the reducing of the blacks to a minimum the appearance of sunshine is obtained. Each pane in the left-hand casement is represented by nothing more than a dot, yet the effect of bright sunshine on a white casement is true enough.

In finding subjects for sketching, many students do not take advantage of different weather conditions for different effects. To these, the fact of it being fairly warm and not raining is sufficient inducement to sit down and draw any view or any building. Yet the first "idea" of a sketch is often a direct result of the weather.

Often a splendid subject is seen from a train window—a fleeting glimpse of a water-mill by a sunny willow-fringed pool, a great grey castle with its bastions reflected in a dark reed-encumbered moat, a twilight impression of a many-roofed town half asleep beneath steep declivity of the downs. All these pictures are "made" by the light and the meteorological conditions.

The water-mill scene on a bright sunshiny day at noon with a high wind blowing will be so different that you will not be able to recognize it. The wind on the water has turned the mill-pond to a grey-blue, and there are no reflections. Your grey castle seen in a bright morning light does not appear to be half so massive as you had thought it, and the blue water rippling among the grasses

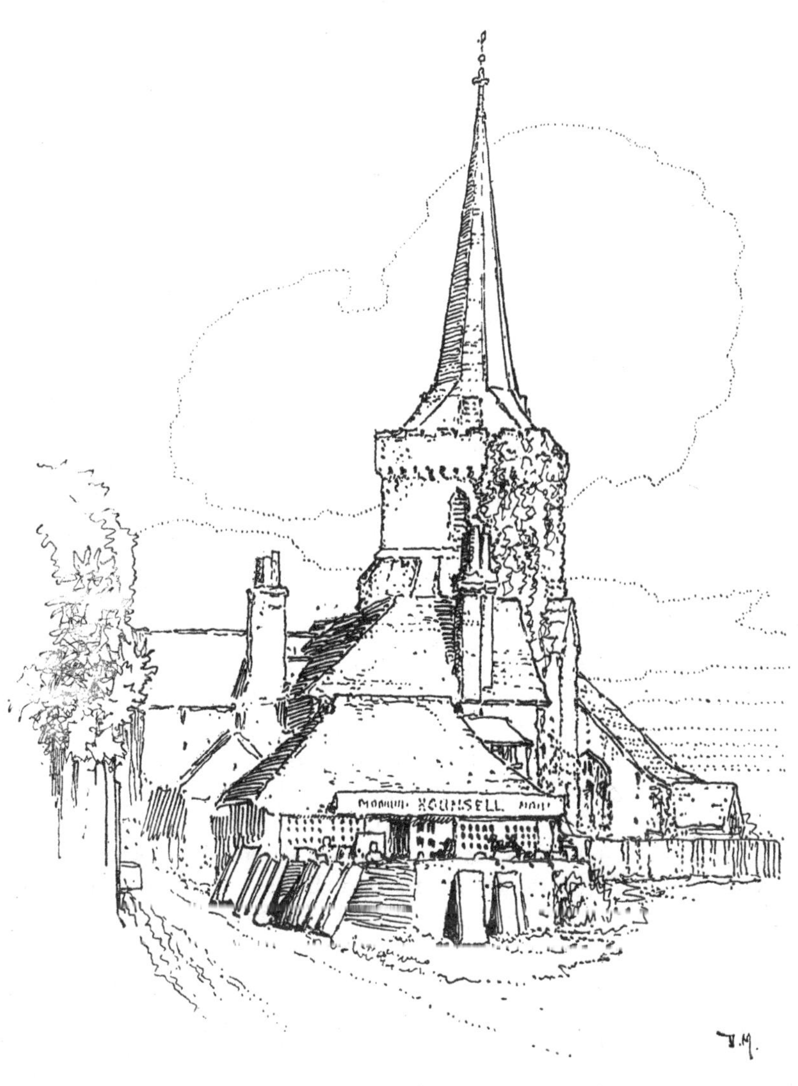

From "Unknown Sussex" (Lane)

CUCKFIELD CHURCH

at the foot of its walls, although pretty enough in itself, does not tend to emphasize the gloom and grandeur of the historic pile. Your many-roofed town under the downs looks rather flippant by bright afternoon light and the dark shapes that suggested medieval castles by twilight are only in reality a mixture of the gasworks and a large brewery.

Where the interest of a subject is in the thing itself, as a picturesque lich-gate, a trestle bridge, or a curious gabled house, rather than in the relation of a number of things one to another in the landscape, then the light does not matter very much. A study of a trestle bridge made on a wet day is as interesting and effective as one made in bright sunshine.

There are subjects, however, that we seek to represent, not so much because of the things themselves, but because they suggest something that they are not. Thus, huge cement works seen through the haze of a misty morning on the Medway will seem to be a giant's castle or a vast creation of Mr. H. G. Wells's imagining in the new Utopia of A.D. 2132. It is necessary to draw this while the day is still misty or all the magic will be gone.

When I was just finishing off my explorations necessitated by writing a book called *Unknown Kent*, I came to Shoreham Mill on a rather dull and muggy afternoon. The dullness, however, was the cause of the exciting factor in the scene, for it made the wooded slopes across the stream come out as an indistinct blue-grey height that suggested something much vaster in the way of forest country than the little valley of the Darent could provide.

A jumble of cottages, heaped timber, wooden sheds, and buildings of the mill all muddled up together as the rough road fell steeply to the water-side came out with curious distinctness against this mysterious background of the woods. The whole scene, for the time, suggested a cameo from the Black Forest or the Vosges. Yet on another day and in a different light the place would look so different that the reader who took this for the place would imagine that I had been romancing.

Part of the equipment of a successful topographical artist is the instant recognition that an effect of light or accident of visibility is making the moment for him to say "Stay!" To represent a place as it is under ordinary and normal conditions is no small

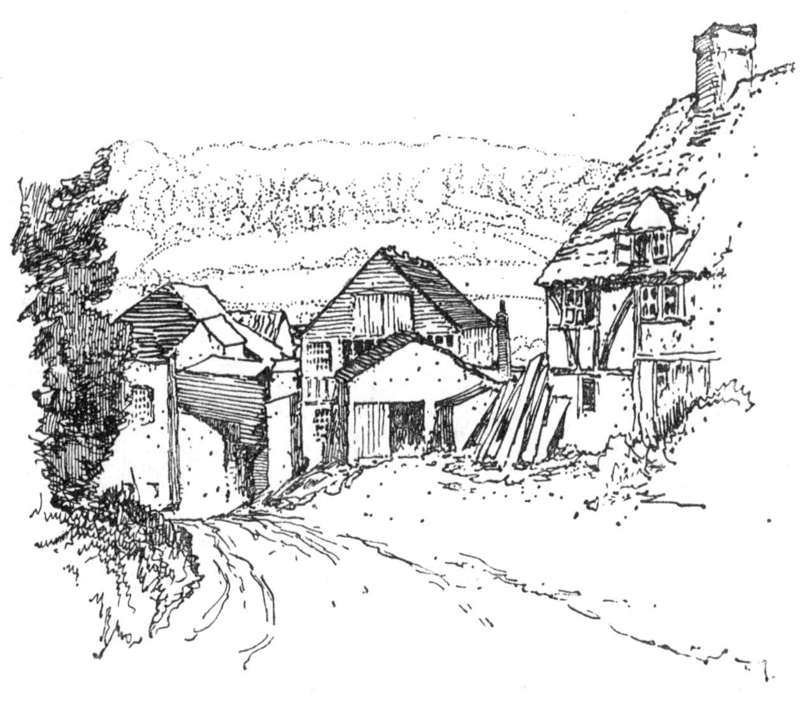

From "Unknown Kent" (Lane)

SHOREHAM MILL, KENT

achievement. To do it well is to add to the accumulative consciousness of Traveller's Joy, for we love to compare one place with another. But best of all is to be able to show some scene or landscape at one of those rare moments when everything conspires together to show its essential character and individual charm.

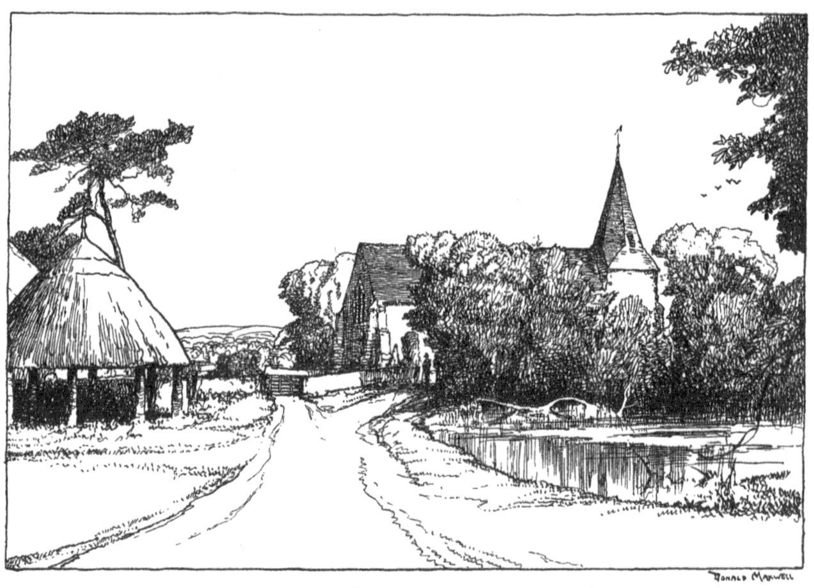

From "A Detective in Sussex" (Lane)

BARCOMBE

PART III

PROBLEMS OF THE DESIGN OF ILLUSTRATIONS WITH A VIEW TO SUCCESSFUL REPRODUCTION

Let me assume by now that the reader is sufficiently confident in expressing himself in pen and ink to look about him for worlds to conquer. He wishes to turn his skill to some professional account and enter this arena of competition, where before the public eye he must fight with editors, publishers, block-makers, printers, printer's devils, and a hundred other devils that will trip him up and render him powerless or make him ridiculous. Many a clever draughtsman has been flattened out, crushed and extinguished by rotary machine printing. It is little consolation for him to go down to his Art Club and discourse on the wickedness of the people who reproduce his work so badly.

The only really intelligent thing he can do is to accept editors, publishers, engravers, paper makers, printers, ink merchants and critics as he must accept the Seven Deadly Sins. It is no use being superior and ignoring their existence. He must fight them.

I have had a very strenuous and varied experience in working for newspapers and illustrating books, and such small measure of success that I may have achieved has been due not to skill in drawing alone but in skill—or in what my enemies would label low cunning—in outmanoeuvring the seven devils to which I have alluded. I hasten to add that these seven devils are only devils in a Pickwickian sense. Editors, publishers, engravers, paper-makers, printers, ink-merchants, and critics, are all my firm friends, and it is to them conspiring with me in good works that I have often been able to turn failure to success under very difficult conditions.

Remember first that a line drawing is printed from a plate that is very much like type. The lines stand up on the plate, which is mounted on wood to the height of the type and in a book all is printed together. In newspaper work, however, and in many books, rotary printing is necessary for the sake of speed. This means that moulds are taken from the type and the blocks and the whole thing is printed from a cylinder. When your delicate line sketch is printed by rotary machinery you must picture it being run off a thing like a steam roller at thousands per hour, on a five mile long ribbon of paper. Little wonder, therefore, that isolated dots in the sky will come out like flying frogs, that thin lines will become thick, black lines appear as grey, and careful cross-hatched shading as solid black.

Let us take a few examples and study them. Both the drawings on page 42 and below were made for reproduction in a newspaper before they were engraved for books. They are no worse for that—as a matter of fact much better, for newspaper work is a great teacher of simplicity and directness of method. Had the birds in

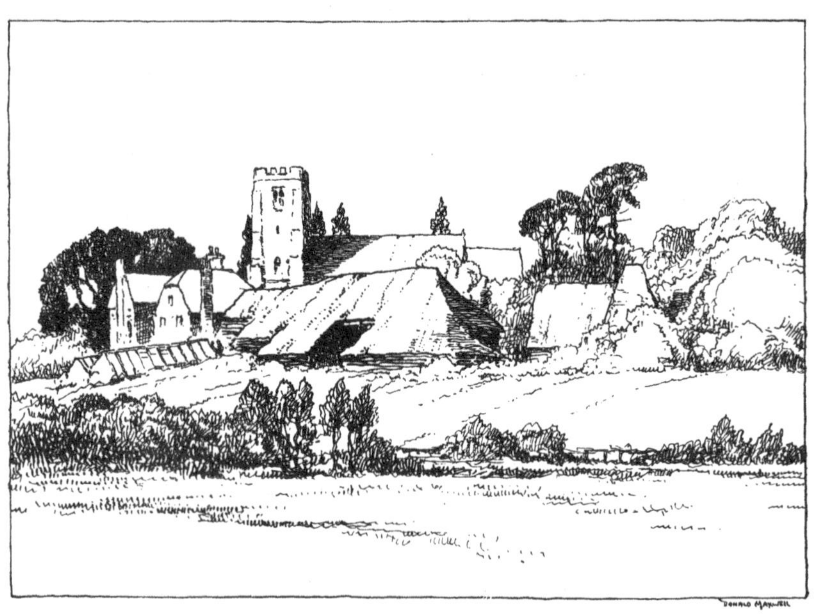

From "A Detective in Sussex" (Lane)

SALEHURST, SUSSEX

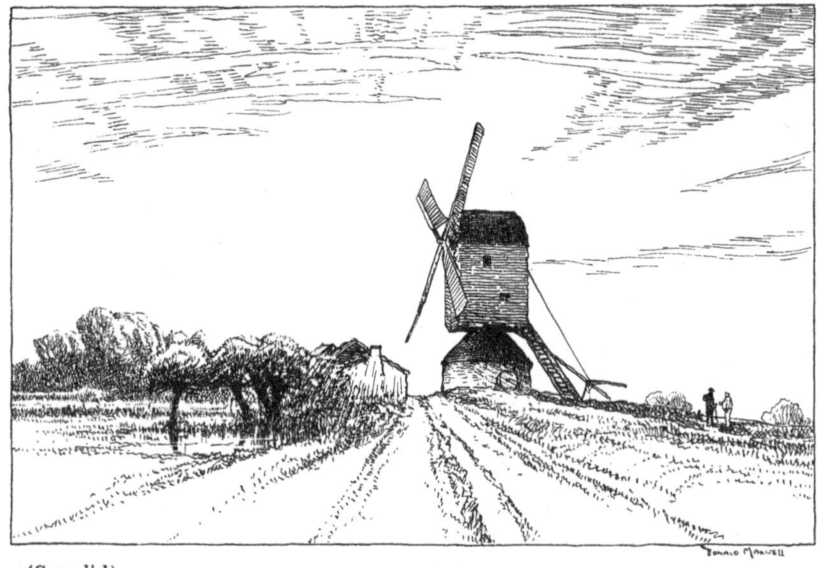

(*Cavendish*)

THE MILL OF MOUNTNESSING

the Barcombe drawing been placed in the middle of the sky instead of in their "protected" position between the church steeple and the foliage on the right they would have appeared as a collision between two aeroplanes. In the Salehurst drawing, likewise, any lines or dots in the sky would have been disastrous.

In newspaper work or in any rapidly printed page or in work necessarily done on "poor" paper, every feature of a drawing will be altered, except one, and that is the paper. The thin line may become a thick one, as we have seen; black lines may become grey and tones fill up solid; but the white spaces of untouched paper in the drawing will remain the same. Thus a successful sketch is one that is composed of a number of white spaces carefully thought out and arranged.

In this sketch of the Mill at Mountnessing such success as it retains in reproduction is on account of white paper. The sun is supposed to be low in the sky at a point about half an inch to the left of the St. Andrew's Cross formed by the sails of the windmill. The lines of the design lead away from this space and thus make a star-like pattern on the paper. I do not mean by this that divergent lines are drawn recklessly to make this star pattern. All these lines represent actual things seen, but those shapes that fit into the scheme are dwelt on, and, where they are unimportant, those that contradict it omitted.

If you will compare this drawing of the mill with the sketch of Rochester Castle on the page opposite you will notice a great difference in treatment. Whereas the mill is a structure that must have a fairly "clean" outline against the sky because it is a piece of mechanism that is working, the ruined keep of Rochester is in a different case. The mill will look a sorry object if its outline is blurred or thickened, but the blunt outline of the castle will be rather improved than otherwise by a little blurring and thickening. Thus the mill is "supported" by lines that take some of the weight of the cylinder as the "attack" of the cylinder is felt, but the castle keep can look after itself and is indeed made more eloquent of ruggedness by its printing defects.

I am trying to show the road to success in pen and ink, and so I must not shirk pointing out the weak spots as well as the strong points of some of the examples given. This sketch of Rochester Castle was made for a newspaper during the Rochester Pageant in the summer of 1931. It was wanted in a great hurry and a direct drawing had to be done for the engraver within a few hours. It is tolerably successful as far as the castle itself is concerned but there is nothing like sufficient contrast between the work in the buildings at the waterside. These should have been treated with a less broken technique. They are too much like the castle in character. This sketch would have been a more vigorous one had it been drawn in the manner of the old Wealden house in the next picture, Burston in the Weald of Kent.

This wonderful old place is a Tudor Mansion hidden in a fold in the parish of Hunton. I made this sketch with a view to it being useful to the compilers of *The New Domesday Book of Kent.* It was first to be published in a newspaper and later as a print, and it presented many difficulties. One general sketch had to suffice to show the rambling place near enough to indicate the half timbering of the back, and yet at such a distance that its position as a farmhouse with its many oast-houses was revealed. Then, to be

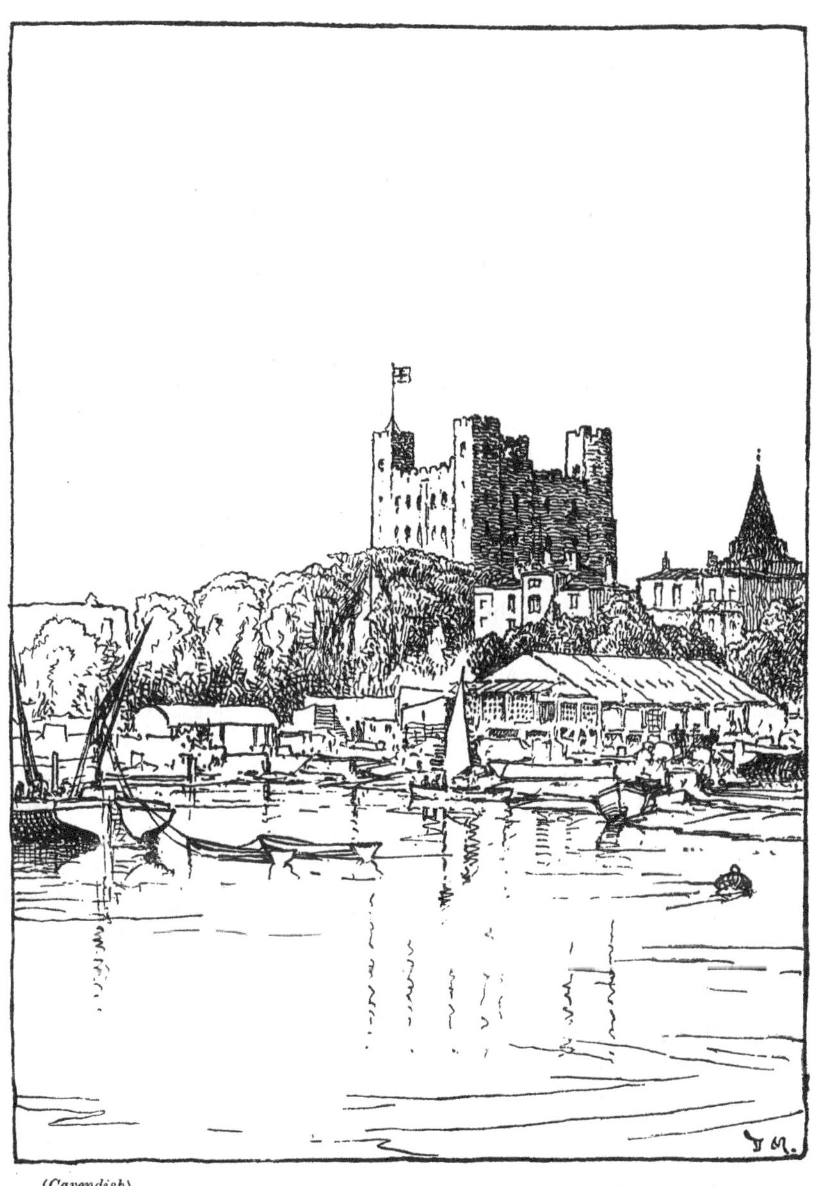

(*Cavendish*)

ROCHESTER CASTLE

true to the facts of this Domesday manor, we must show its position on the hillside overlooking the trench of the Weald, a vast prospect bounded by the distant hills that overlook the sea.

How is all this to be shown in one small drawing? It is a problem but not an insoluble one. Remember that more battles have been lost by want of good generalship than by want of bravery. What we must do is to manoeuvre for position.

Unless the printing of a subject like this is very good there will be difficulty in showing a delicate and complicated distance in contrast to a vigorous foreground. The lines of the distant work will tend to coarseness by inking and pressure if they are in an isolated position on the paper. However, if these distant lines are intersected by strong foreground objects, such as tree trunks cutting across them, their delicacy will be saved. The heavy lines of the tree work will take the weight of the cylinder and thus the fine lines will not be over-inked or over-impressed.

I walked miles up and down hill and viewed Burston from every conceivable angle before I settled down to the view I have depicted. By getting the oast-houses so that they overtopped the horizon on the left and by using an apple tree to advantage on the right, I protected the delicate distance and thus maintained some of the effect of recession in the vast *campagne* that Kipling would call "the blue goodness of the Weald." You may think, possibly, that I have over-laboured the point about indifferent printings, and that bitter experience has developed in me what psychologists call a complex. Nothing could be farther from the truth. I have often worked for publishers who see to it that the printing they do is quite perfect. However, I recognize that the experience I have obtained in negotiating the difficulties of bad printing have stood me in good stead even when the reproduction is excellent. It is difficult to say why exactly; I suppose it is that dodging difficulties and pitfalls teaches the artist never to draw without thinking. Drawing without thinking has been the downfall of many a clever penman who at last develops a facile technique of which the public soon tires.

I remember once having a pupil who developed this fatal facility. He found a ready and effective way of expressing tiled roofs and old brick walls. Everything that had any likeness to

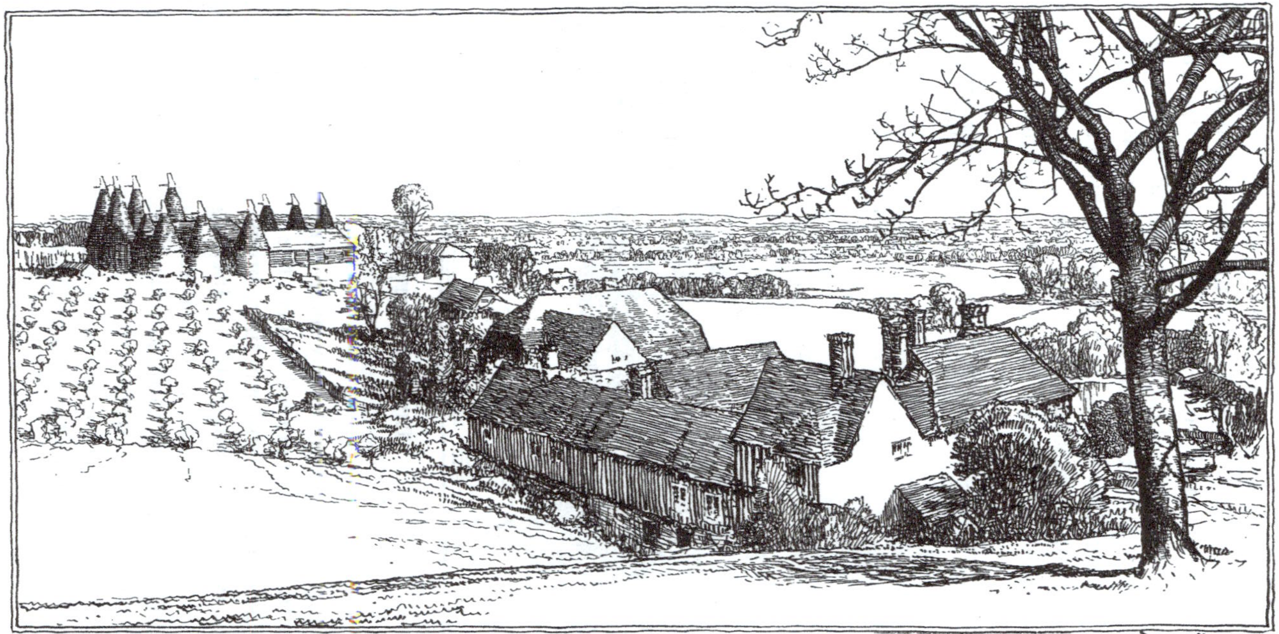

(*Cavendish*)

BURSTON, IN THE WEALD OF KENT

inches and came out very well. As shown here, however, it is still further reduced to four inches and a quarter, and is quite bright and clear. It could be reduced to two inches wide or even less and be a coherent picture. In like manner, the sketch of Copman Thorpe in the snow could be reduced down to the size of a postage stamp and still show the main points of the picture. Probably the sky would fill up to a solid black. Even in that event the road, the church, the village cross, and the snow-covered trees would be discernible. The original sketch of this subject, like that of Rochester, is thirteen inches in width.

Judging from the effects we see in book illustrations and other drawings, many artists, and some of these by no means beginners, have great difficulty in representing reflections in water. A most depressing and forlorn aspect is given to a riverside sketch, or a lake scene, if there is an appearance of sodden chopped straw floating about. Many a sketch by Thames side can I recall that is almost masterly in its treatment of architecture and overhanging trees, but this wretched chopped straw will flop about and spoil everything.

The remedy for this unfortunate state of things is not far to seek. It is necessary for us to get clear in our minds exactly what constitutes a reflection of an object in the water. It is said of Turner that he once spent a whole day throwing stones in a pond in order to study the nature of reflections.

A reflection is the exact image of a thing as seen from the level of the water. Only in absolutely calm water is this image exact. You have, no doubt, seen river photographs that might be printed either way up with little clue as to what is the reality and what the reflection.

Various circumstances alter this image: a strong breeze rippling the water may break up its surface so that there is no reflection at all. The reflected image may be broken in places only or it may be entirely distorted in pattern, but always with some broken likeness to the thing reflected.

No reflection will look right in a picture that does not recognize exactly the shape of the object above it. For instance, in the winter sketch on the Medway, the bridge is reflected in a very broken and exaggerated manner. Roughly speaking, only the vertical facts are reflected and those in rather an elongated way.

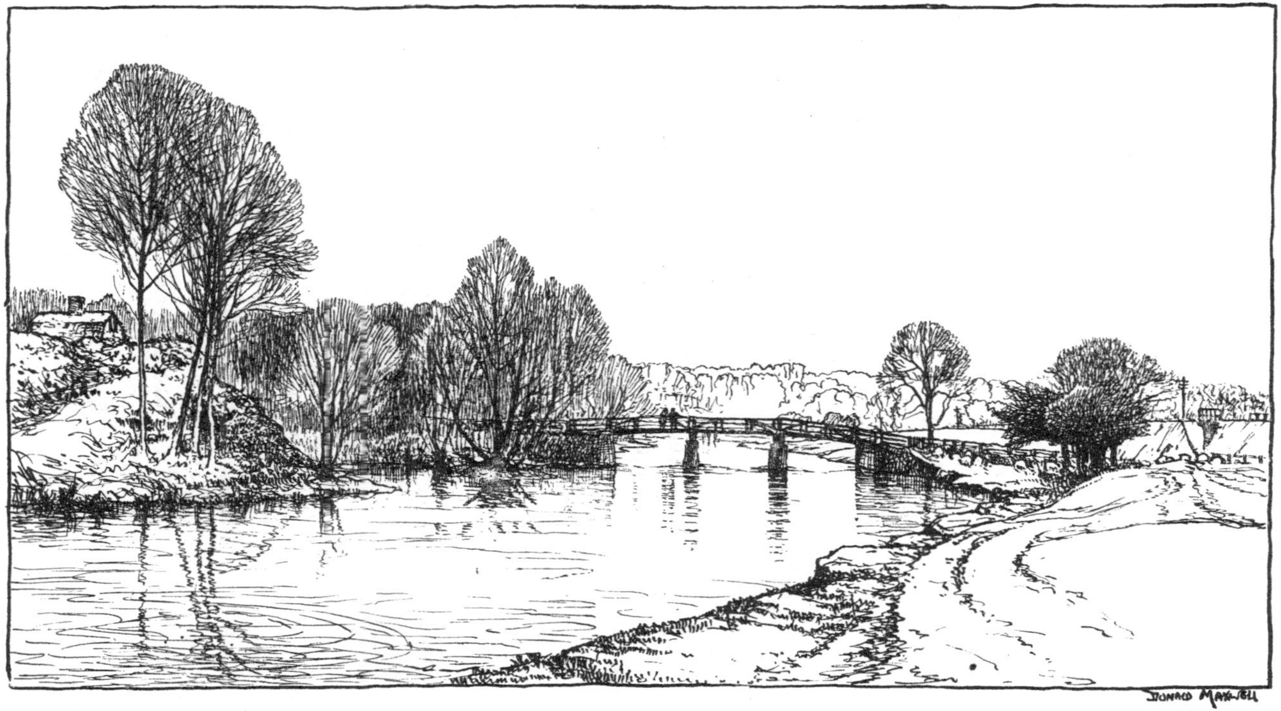

DONALD MAXWELL

(Cavendish)

A Winter Landscape on the Medway

The rails and footway of the bridge have disappeared and only the piers and sides of the brickwork, and the two figures on the bridge are accounted for at all. Observe, however, that it is *exactly* underneath these things that horizontal marks make up what can be seen of the image of the bridge. These in still water may be immensely extended, sometimes right down to the feet of the spectator standing on the bank, *but all these marks will be exactly* underneath the thing reflected. A T-square should be used if necessary to ensure accuracy.

Now let us take the group of four trees on the left hand side of the picture and see what we are going to do about their reflections in the water. The fact that the water is moving all the time is not really so great a difficulty as it at first appears. All this movement is within certain very clearly defined zones.

In order to get these reflections right, I took a tracing of the four trees, and then made an horizontal line in pencil at a point about an eighth of an inch above the line of the water's edge. This is to get the right plane of reflection. If we were to cut away the bank to the trees this would be the reflecting point. Then I turned it upside down and thus carefully outlined the trees in pencil in the water as if they made a perfectly clear and still reflection. Within the pencil boundaries of these reflected tree-trunks, a few broken dashes or wriggling lines, *kept always strictly within the boundaries set by the outline,* will give the effect of reflection in the slightly rippling and flowing water.

The other reflection, that of the tree at the water's edge to the left of the bridge, was arrived at in the same way. Two zones of white marks, caused by the wind, break this at two points, but such little reflection of branches as still remains strictly follows the outline of the tree above.

The most difficult effects in pen and ink, and those generally least successful in published work, are effects of light and dark tone over a large surface. They are also very laborious and it is a temptation to take mechanical short cuts by means of engravers' dotted or line-tones. These are generally unsatisfactory and *look* mechanical, except in the hands of exponents of line work, who are far beyond needing any tips in a technical work of this kind.

The night sketch here of Peterborough Cathedral from the

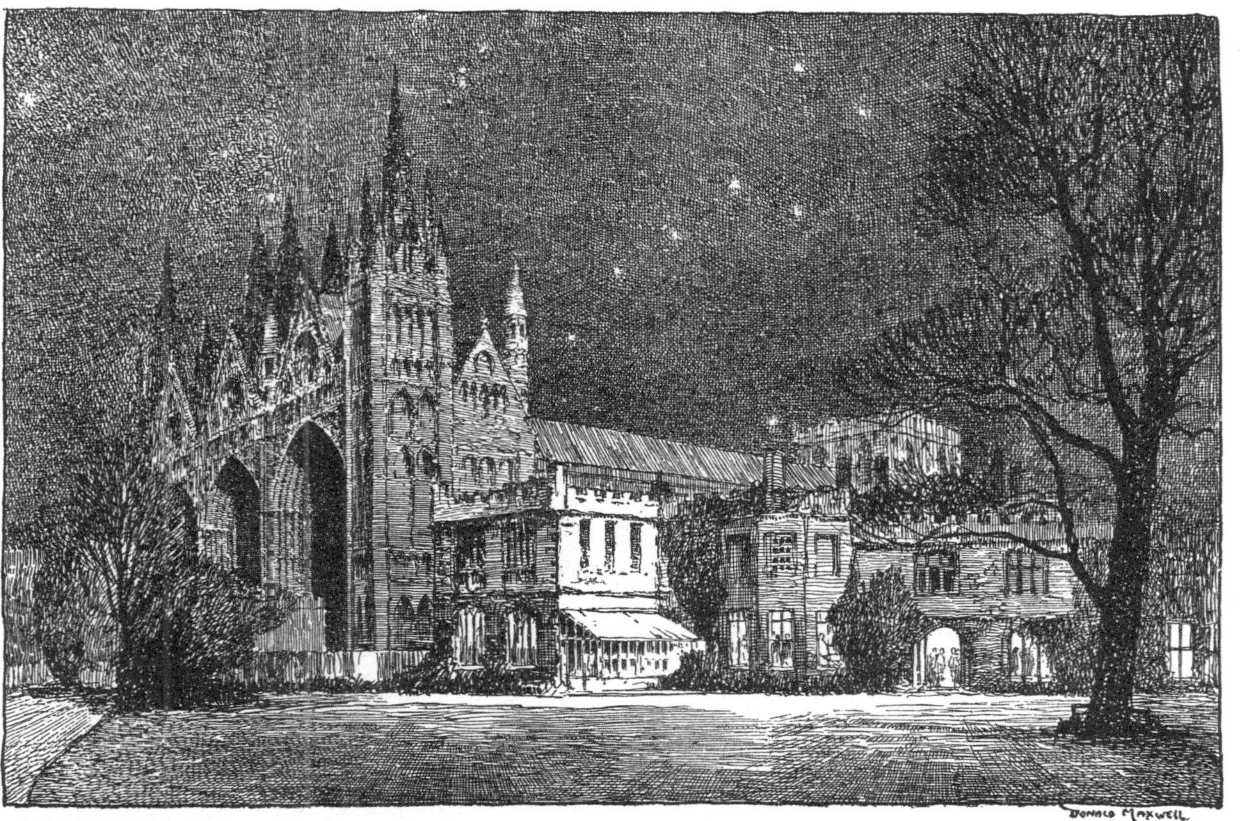

("*Church Times*")

A Nocturne of Peterborough Cathedral

gardens of the Bishop's Palace was made for *The Church Times*, and the original drawing was about seventeen inches in diameter. It was reduced to twelve inches in width and came out well for newspaper printing. The block printed here was engraved not from the original drawing, but from a newspaper cutting, so that you can see that the line work is still as clear as in the original drawing, although reduced to six and a quarter inches in width. This is a big reduction, 17 to 6, far more than desirable, but it establishes the fact that a drawing built up on right lines retains some merit even when abused.

The next drawing, a moonlight of Exeter Cathedral, is another seventeen-inch wide drawing which is here purposely over-reduced. In this case it is knocked down from seventeen to four and a quarter, a frightful abuse of editorial power, yet some eloquence has remained in it. True the sky, now filled up to black in places, clings round the Cathedral in an unpleasant manner, and there is little of the broad moonlight effect left. Yet, because the lights on the building were drawn in a very open manner, there is still some glamour and glitter of silvery light surviving to tell the tale.

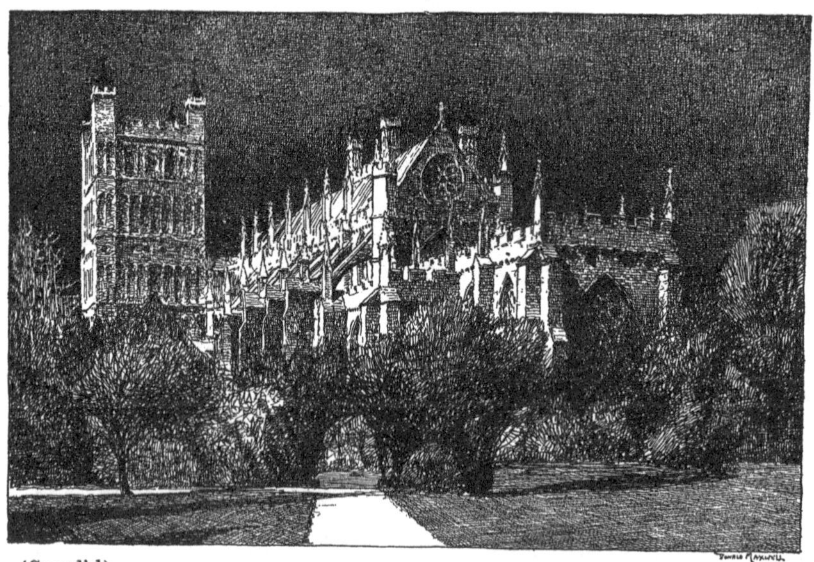

(Cavendish)

EXETER CATHEDRAL

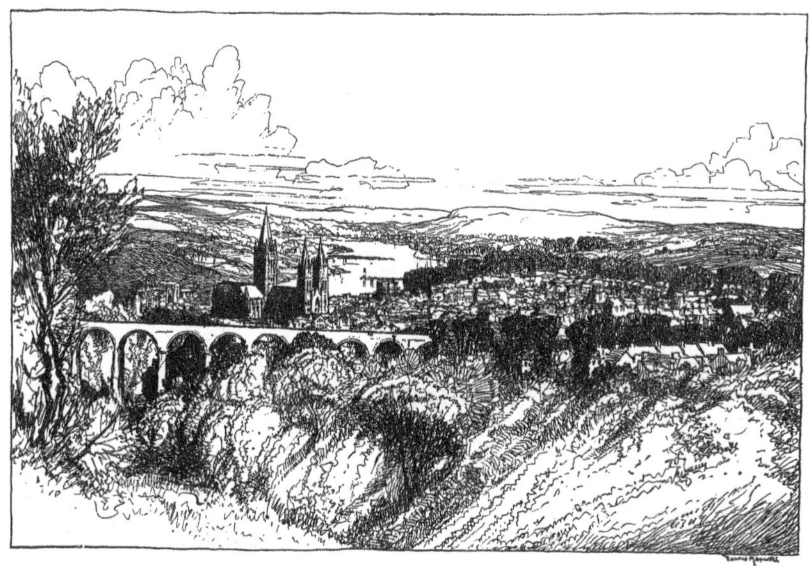

(*Cavendish*)

TRURO

In a large drawing like the one of Peterborough, great care must be taken with the choice of pattern for a surface of tone. This sketch, being night, must be toned nearly all over. There are three component parts of the tone work. There is the sky; there are buildings and there is a surface of lawn. The tree is practically solid black, so that texture question does not occur here.

I should suggest to the craftsman that he should think out the problem something on the lines I am about to indicate, but it is not at all necessary that he should use the same "patterns" as I have found expressive.

Sky. The sky is of substance and quality, different from everything else in the picture. Some pattern, not too noticeable, should be devised to represent this in contrast to any other pattern in the sketch.

Buildings. All buildings might well be represented with definite lines following shapes as in roof and in bay of Palace.

Lawn. Some pattern to express surface: something different from buildings and sky.

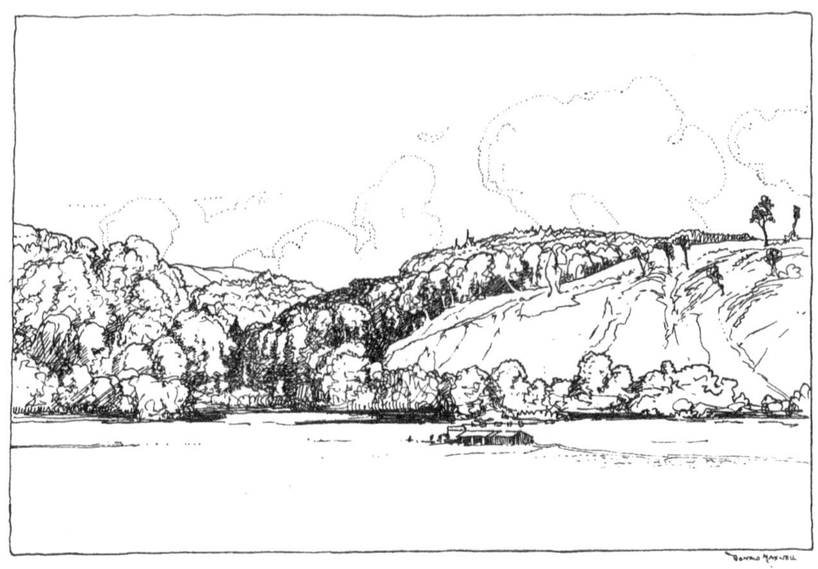

(*Lane*)

A SKETCH FROM "THE BOOK OF THE CLYDE"

The drawing of Truro, on page 57, is another example of work originally drawn for reproduction on a larger scale, but retaining some merit by means of careful planning of light and shade.

The original sketch was, as in Peterborough, seventeen inches in width, to be reproduced twelve inches wide, and here further reduced to four and a quarter. In this twelve-inch print the shadowed side of the towers, nave and transept of the Cathedral are in open cross-hatched line, but they have filled up to solid black. This possibility was anticipated and the very light and open work of the distance is sufficiently slight, even in this much over-reduced print, not to swamp the Cathedral in lines and heavy tone, and obliterate it. The shadow zones of trees have also become practically black, but this does not alter the general composition of the picture or its clearness.

And now it is necessary to say something to the sketcher on the difficulties of sky effects and the problem of what to put in and what to leave out. The tendency for him is to put in the sky that he sees at the moment. This is more possible to the painter than to the sketcher in pen and ink. Often heavy clouds and passages of tone will spoil a line sketch. I hear the captious critic exclaim: "Why cannot an artist put in what he sees; why all this modification and alteration?"

The answer is a very complex one, and I do not know, with all the experience I have had in pen sketching, that I can answer it with any degree of confidence or satisfaction.

In the first place, there are no lines at all in most of the things we see in a landscape. There are no lines in the sky or upon the shadow-chequered downs or in the sun that goes down in a fume of gold. At the best, lines are often only a convention or an abstraction to show the shape of something or the tendencies of its many surfaces. This limitation is felt mostly in drawing sea and sky by the pen and ink artist who has nothing with which to represent waves and clouds but lines—of which in nature there are none. But take heart. Truth is many-sided. We cannot represent all things with the pen, but we can represent some. We cannot

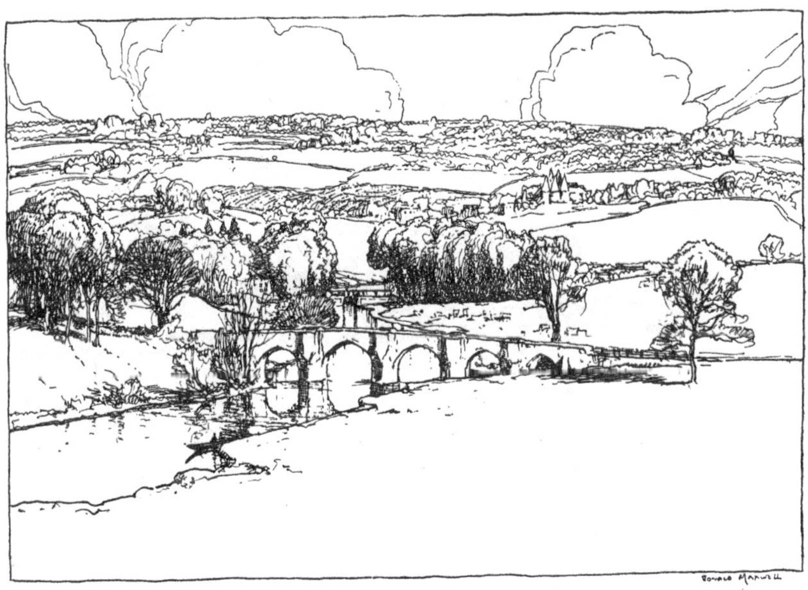

From "More Adventures among Churches" (Faith Press)

A MEDIEVAL BRIDGE ON THE MEDWAY

draw a "deceptive illusion" of a cloud, but we can say something of its shape, its buoyancy, its movement, and not a little of its glory.

Perhaps it would be helpful in attacking this problem of skies to compare the three drawings in this part of the book: "Truro," a sketch from *The Book of the Clyde*, and "A Medieval Bridge on the Medway." In the first of these the distant rising cumulus clouds are indicated in outline. The drawing is such an elaborate one and so strong in blacks that these do not overweight the sky.

In the Clyde sketch, however, which shows nothing but confused outlines of trees and hills, clouds as in the Truro or Medway drawings would be fatal. Their shapes are too much the shapes of the trees, and they might look like great trees themselves. The similarity of the dome shape of trees and the dome shape of clouds would not matter in a water-colour drawing because the colour and tonal contrast would be so great that there would be no confusion.

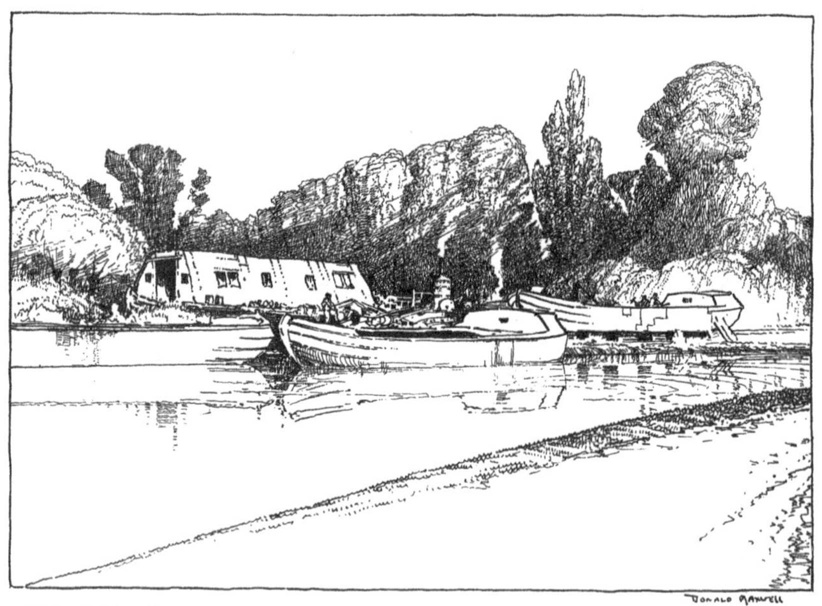

("*Church Times*")

A SHIPYARD IN ARCADY

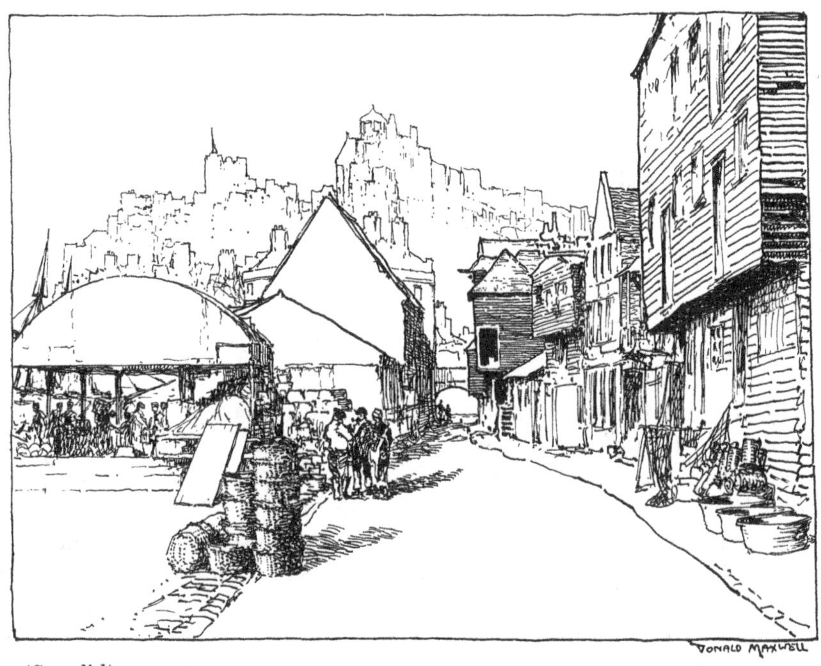

(*Cavendish*)

FOLKESTONE FISH MARKET

To meet this possible ambiguity of effect I drew the clouds in dotted lines, and thus they take on a buoyant quality and become airy and detached from the hilly sky line. Not so in the Medway sketch. Here the definite interest of the bridge and flatter landscape holds the eye and the billowy clouds appear as heavy and even solid looking things, but sufficiently of the sky order of things not to confuse the landscape. I might mention in making these comparisons that the artifice of using a vague and dotted outline to clouds is one that could only be used when the printing is to be good. This Clyde drawing was made for a book illustration. In quick newspaper printing there would be a danger of the dotted line joining up into one solid and continuous line and thus the artifice would become useless.

And now, putting aside for the moment the difficulties and

dangers of bad printing, let us study together further problems of selection and representation in sketching. There is nothing so useful as the continual habit of selecting subjects when you are prospecting with a sketch book. Many of these selections are never likely to be taken any farther, but it is a good habit to make a quick and scribbled memorandum of a possible picture. The very best pictures are sometimes to be seen from trains or under conditions when it is impossible to stop. However, a note made in ten seconds is often of use in building up a composition. The hobby of picture making is an accumulative study and very soon you will be able to see "pictures" in the most unlikely places.

One of the most unexpected subjects that it has been my good fortune to find was on the Grand Junction Canal, near West Drayton. I suddenly came upon Noah's Ark in all its glory. It was being used as a carpenter's shop in a waterside depot for painting and repairing canal boats. Beside it, in the morning sun, lay boats with bows and sterns freshly adorned in all the colours of the rainbow. I immediately thought of a happy title—a great incentive to completing a drawing expressive of a certain mood—and called it "A Shipyard in Arcady."

It is often useful in a very confused and complicated subject, as in some lights is the Fish Market at Folkestone, to practise some degree of omission of detail, and yet—being in the nature of a portrait—the facts of the view, with all its over-richness of detail will have to be faced.

It is a good plan to draw everything that you can see in a careful pencil drawing and then to fill in some features in tone with light and shade, and others in outline only. In a place like Folkestone Fish Market smoke and sea mists will often help you. In this sketch I have filled in only the outline of a few features of the town and then drawn the nearer houses in full light and shade.

I do not propose to go into questions of technique in drawing the sea because he who can manage a lee shore or the chop of wind against tide will not need any hints from me. I will rather keep to those subjects that are within the compass of teachability. The moving storm, the crumbling wave, and the wreathing vapours of twilight are all subjects beyond tuition.

Let us rather walk together beside the waters of the Medway.

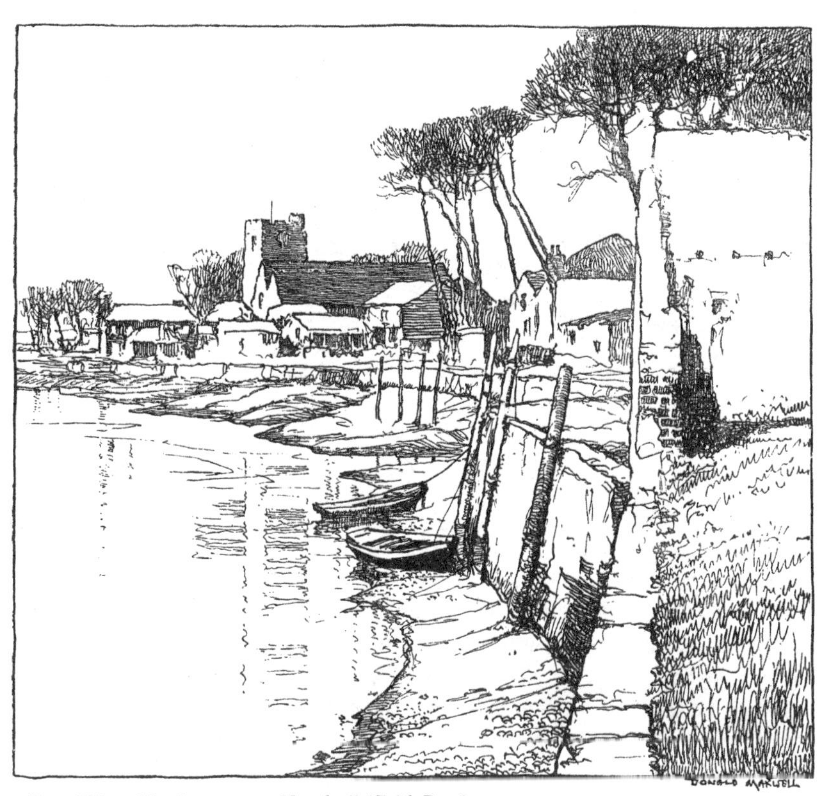

From "More Adventures among Churches" (Faith Press)

WOULDHAM, ON THE MEDWAY

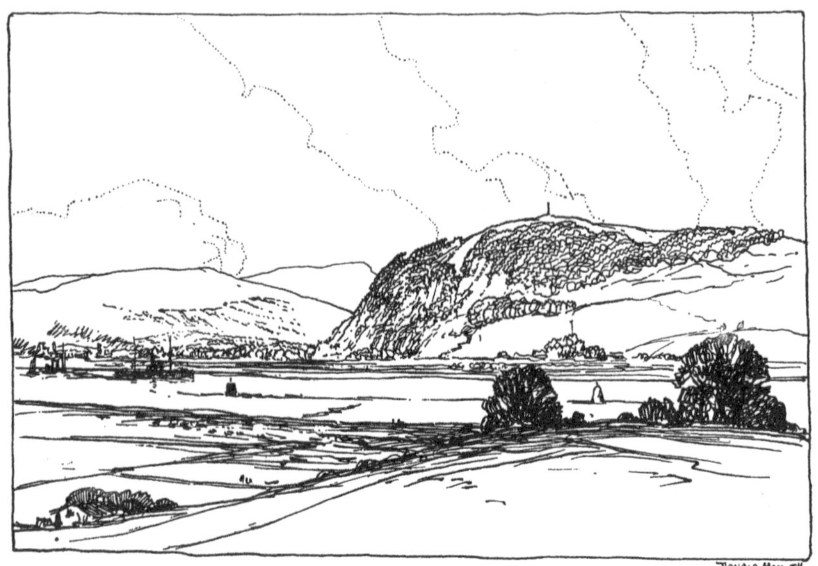

From "The Book of the Clyde" (Lane)

DUMBUCK

Milton has called the Medway "Medway smooth," so placidity is evidently a recognized quality of its nature. The Medway shores will keep reasonably still while we study them.

We come to Wouldham, and, choosing a position on a somewhat decrepit quay, look downstream towards the church. The tide has ebbed sufficiently to strand two boats, and the water is calm enough to give us an easy time with reflections.

These reflections are easy. A few wriggling lines will express the sheet of placid water *so long as the wriggling marks are exactly underneath the things reflected.*

However, if we are not careful, we may give the effect of a large pond. Of course the boats show that it is a river rather than a pond, but we must provide something more than this circumstantial evidence. We must make people who look at the drawing *feel* that the river is flowing. Therefore it is necessary to look for lines and shapes and arrangements of objects that suggest rhythm, succession, and gentle movement.

The line of the tops of the trees, the tide line of the mud, and the line of the quay-side all conspire to help. We will seize on them whatever else we leave out. Then the succession of bare tree-trunks and the echoing procession of posts in diminishing size give this idea of motion. All these things are there and it is an exact and true topographical document, but by emphasis we have made it into a picture also.

The placing of a good black mass somewhere in a line drawing, often supported by a lesser black, is a great help to the decorative effect of the whole design. In the Wouldham sketch the shadow of the broken wall does a lot to compose the subject, and this is supported by the lesser black of the boat. In the sketches of Dumbuck and Offham that come next are blacks that key up the subjects to some extent—in the former subject the black trees of the middle distance and in the latter the tall Scotch fir.

The drawing of Dumbuck presented the same difficulty about the lines of the clouds and their possible confusion with the lines of the hills, as the other sketch on the Clyde, on page 58, and as that too was for a book illustration and one that would be well

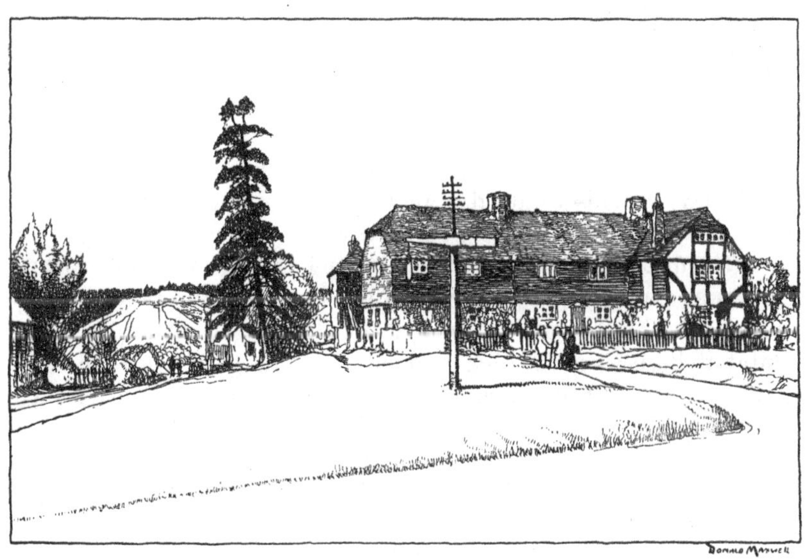

(*Cavendish*)

MEDIEVAL OFF AM

printed I got out of the difficulty in the same way by outlining the clouds in dots.

In all illustration work the pen and ink artist will be up against a great many difficulties of which the people that employ him know nothing. He will be asked to draw very new looking things—such as buildings handsomely restored—to look old, because they *are* old, and he will be asked to portray a comparatively insignificant object in a large view so that it looks important. I had two such problems, and two sketches here, "Offham" and "The Oldest Inn of Norwich," show the difficulties encountered and only in one case, I fear, overcome.

The drawing of Offham depicts the village green on which stands a thing which at first sight appears to be a signpost. It is not a signpost, however, but a quintain—the only one, I am told, in England. I do not know exactly how the thing worked, but I have been told that it held a sack of sawdust, depending from one arm and exhibited a disc on the other. A horseman with lance tilted at the disc and registered a *hit.* If he missed he was covered with confusion, but if he struck the bull's-eye according to plan he had to be very nimble in ducking for the sack of sawdust would swing round and unhorse him unless he pressed forward in the half-second of grace.

I was unwise in attempting too much. I tried to combine a view of the village green and its old houses and the quintain also. On the larger scale of its first production the quintain came out clearly, but on this reduced scale it is too mixed up with the roof of the cottages. The weight, painted white, which now hangs from the left arm of this strange device in place of the sack of sawdust, appears as part of the window behind it. From the point of view from which this sketch was made the drawing is a failure, and I exhibit it here as a warning and in the same grim spirit of satisfaction as the temperance lecturer does when he produces the awful example.

The other drawing, "The Oldest Inn of Norwich," has succeeded in a greater measure. The difficulty I had to face here was the fact that the oldest inn of Norwich at first sight did not appear to be so particularly old. Probably it wasn't. It had been re-roofed no doubt, and partially rebuilt, and it is generally the interior of

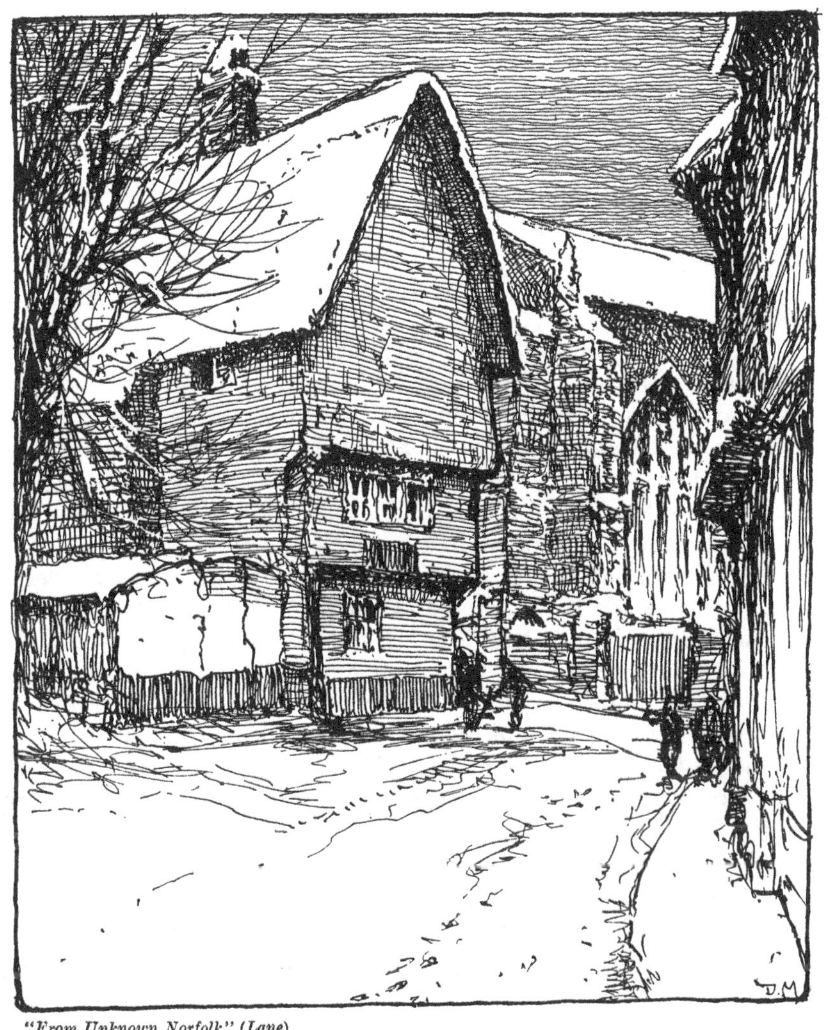

"From Unknown Norfolk" (*Lane*)

THE OLDEST INN OF NORWICH

such buildings that exhibit their oldest features. I therefore sought for a treatment that, while doing no violence to the topographical accuracy of the scene, might make my drawing of the inn *look* as though it might be the oldest inn of the city.

A touch of snow was my chance. This helped to give a more ancient quality to the roof, and a Gothic window, loaded with snow could be brought into the view to complete the illusion. Plastered with drifted snow, some very prosaic buildings on the right did not obtrude themselves and all went well. Footsteps in the white foreground might suggest good King Wenceslas passing as any one else, and so a complete medieval picture in the streets of Norwich to-day was possible, and in it was nothing but the truth.

Note also as you build up your technique for illustration work that the nature of your toning can have a very great deal to do with the success of the drawing. In any case, to show up the snow in the most distant building, there will have to be a considerable amount of shading. If this were done with a succession of planes of neat paralleled lines this would no doubt render the architectural facts of the building correctly, but—except in the hands of a skilful draughtsman—the building would not appear to be very old. The carelessly distributed and rugged lines on the gable of the inn, lines that have "bad joints" and omissions, in this sketch greatly accentuate the appearance of rough plaster fissured and uneven, with here and there a dust of snow on some protuberance.

Beware of many solid blacks in a drawing unless you are certain that it is going to be well printed. They have a knack of going gray and nothing is so depressing as a starred and mealy-looking black. The next example I want to show you is "Aladdin in Ipswich," which was designed for an illustration for my book, "Unknown Suffolk." I knew it would be well reproduced and so used a solid black sky to show up the grain towers—at least I supposed them to be grain elevators—and give the whole place the appearance of the magic castle in the pantomime.

It is a thing worth remembering that as a rule a drawing is most likely to be successful in its effect when its principal objects are consistently lighter or darker than the sky behind them. Also it is well to note that fine points like the details of a Gothic building

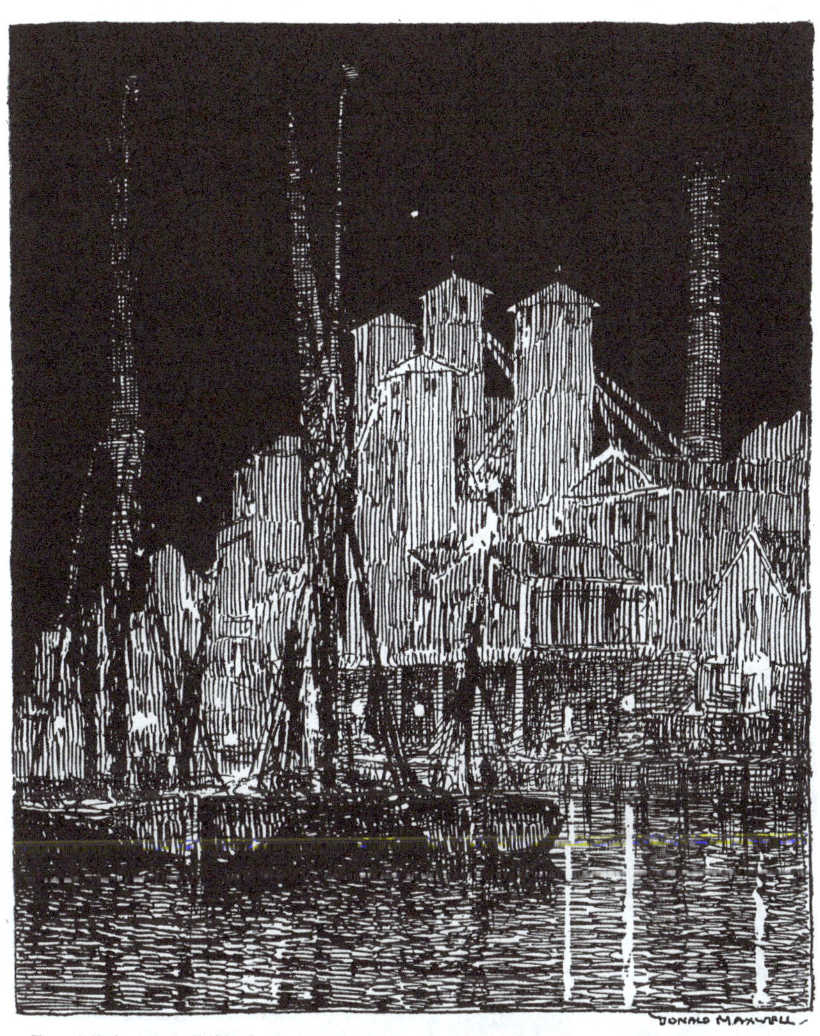

From "Unknown Suffolk" (Lane)

ALADDIN IN IPSWICH

are less likely to get "damaged" or coarsened when they are light against dark than when they are dark against light. In the sketch, "Canterbury in Snow," the pinnacles of the various towers of the Cathedral are seen crisp and delicate against the black of the night sky. Had the scheme of light and shade been as in the "Guston" drawing, i.e. the pinnacles sticking up into a white sky, these would probably have been coarsened or blunted.

Note, too, that the very different treatment of the light and shade in these two sketches, "Canterbury" and "Guston," is justified, if my judgment in the matter be right, by the result. The great mass of Canterbury Cathedral, although here small and at some distance, can take care of itself. It is sufficiently intricate and important to dominate the sky-line.

The little church of Guston, however, treated in that way would be "swamped" by the sky, whereas, as seen here, its simple lines are effective against the clear white above it.

Now we come to the last example in this section in our attempts to solve technical problems. This really belongs to the next part

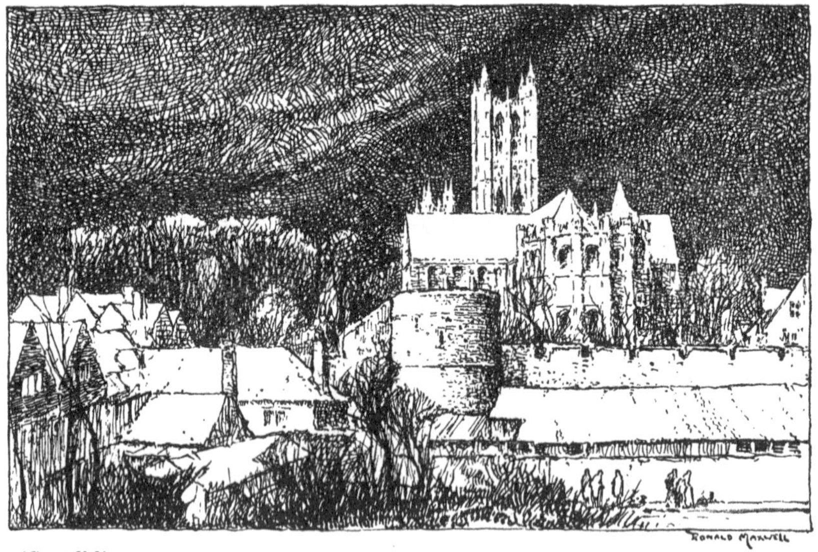

(Cavendish)

CANTERBURY IN SNOW

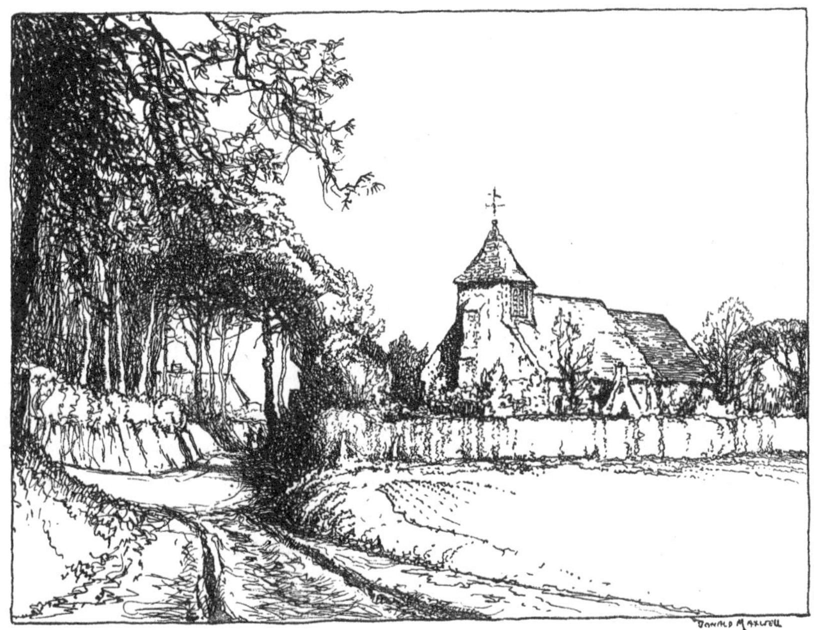

("*Church Times*")

GUSTON, NEAR DOVER

of the book, for the problem was one more of archaeology than of printing.

I set myself to show in one drawing that Canterbury, for all its medieval and modern rebuilding, is really a visible continuation of the old Roman-planned city.

The High Street of Canterbury is not the old Watling Street that ran straight from Dover to London, south-east and north-west, but it is more or less parallel to that ancient highway. The gridiron formation of the city's ways, parallel with or at right-angles to the streets of the Roman town, are maintained. Thus the city is four-square, north-west, south-west, south-east and north-east.

From the top of St. Dunstan's Church, from which point I made this sketch, the town-planning of the Romans is apparent. The only exception to this square "lay-out" is the Cathedral. The Cathedral was a late comer and although built, north, east, south, west, nothing else in the town follows its lines. It stands at an angle of forty-five degrees to the rest of Canterbury.

A drawing like this to the uninitiated looks very complicated and difficult, but it is really very simple. Let it be admitted it is laborious and accounts for a considerable amount of time, but that is not the same thing as being difficult. If you can draw one house and one church, you can draw a city.

From the technical point of view, in case you have never tried a subject like this, I will try and suggest the best method of attack. First rule a pencil line for the horizon and then rule a few more pencil lines underneath it at intervals. Then with a set-square mark off a good many vertical lines in pencil, dropping down from this horizon line to the foot of the picture, also put in vanishing point lines as in Fig. 5 on page 7. These will be useful to act as a guide when you come to drawing the details of houses, which otherwise—such is my experience—will fall about and give the appearance of a frightful earthquake in full progress.

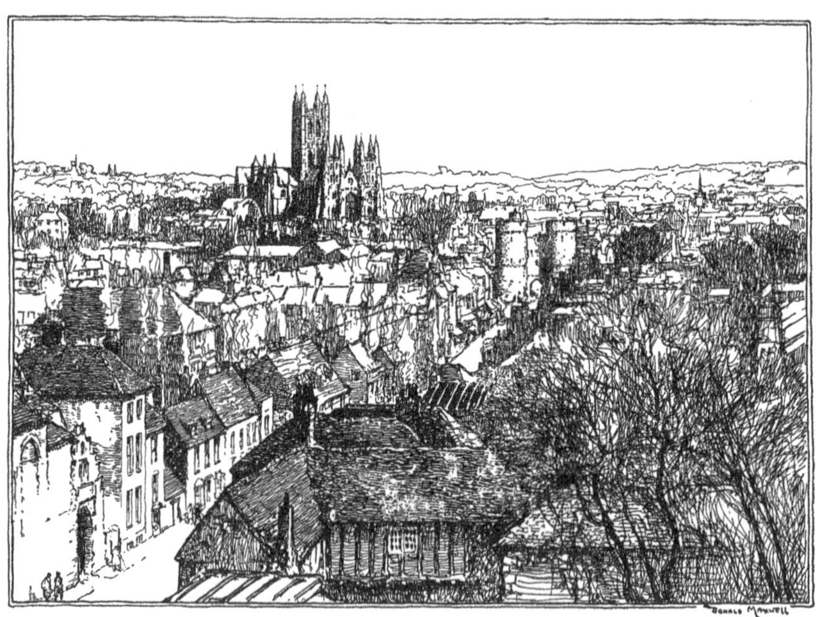

(*Cavendish*)

CANTERBURY FROM THE WEST

PART IV

PROBLEMS OF INTERPRETATION AND OF THE IMAGINATIVE TREATMENT OF SKETCHING IN PEN AND INK

WE must now assume that the reader is no longer a beginner. He has to some extent mastered the means of expression in line. He has evolved some technique of his own, and he has learned to make himself eloquent in spite of rotary printing and dreadful conditions which at first reduced his speech to a stammer.

In fact this part of my little book is meant for those who are out for adventure. It deals with higher problems than those of representation and mechanics. It deals in fact—forgive the paradox—with the mechanics of poetry. You are no longer content to be a conveyance (to borrow a simile from Ruskin) and take your readers to a place and leave them to their own conclusions about it. You wish to go with them and talk to them and enthuse them with things that you see—things indeed that most of them will not see without you. Mr. Terrick Williams once said to me: "Really, a picture is not of the best sort unless it is clear that the artist sees something that no one else sees."

This statement is a witty expression of a profound philosophy in picture making. Its truth is apparent if you will think of any painting of great charm. Turner's "Fighting Temeraire," Whistler's "Nocturne in Blue and Silver," or Cotman's 'Wherries on the Yare"—to take three well-known landscapes in the National Gallery—are all examples of pictures in which the artist has seen something that no one else would have seen. Of course, we can all see it now—as post-Columbus scientists have all been able to balance hard-boiled eggs on their ends—but these masters have opened another door of observation for us.

With this preamble, I should like to disclaim all sense of superiority of method and write for my artists of adventure—press and illustration—as one experimenter to another. Some of my experiences will amuse you and some may give you ideas when you are up against the same problems.

Pen and ink is before all other things the perfect medium for illustration. In the first place, it is the cheapest method of picture-printing in books, can go in with the text and is the only one that will give an exact image of the artist's work. Line for line, and dot for dot, the reader is looking at the picture itself and not at a translation.

Pen and ink is not only the perfect medium for illustration —it *is* illustration. During a long and varied career as an artist, I have been commissioned to draw all sorts of places in many parts of the world, but only once have I been asked to do a drawing of a scene in pen and ink for the sake of the thing itself and not for reproduction.

Well, now for problems and adventures. The two next sketches are from a series of travel articles that saw the light as "Adventures with a Sketch-book." They concern the voyage of a barge by

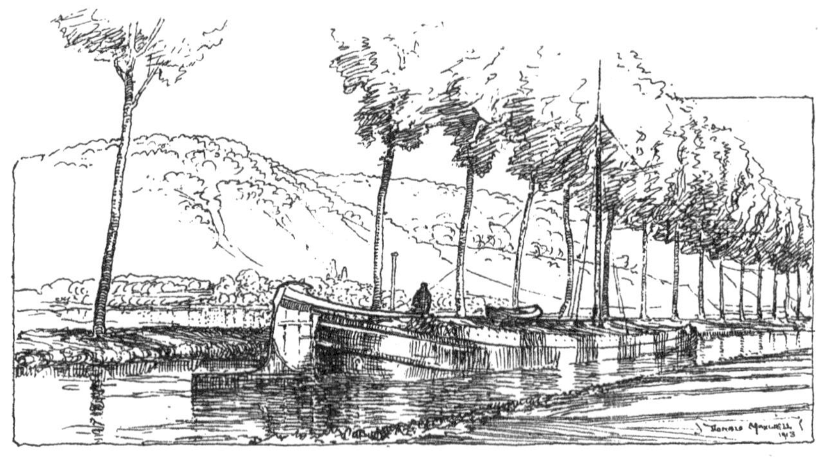

From "Adventures with a Sketch-book" (Lane)

NEAR LIVERDUN

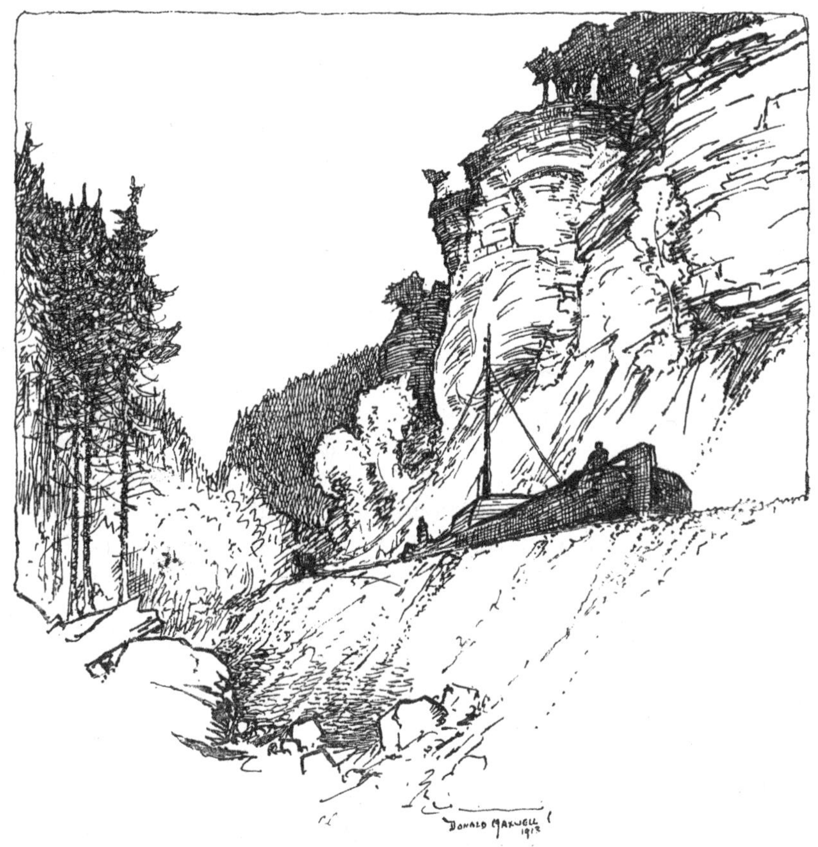

From "Adventures with a Sketch-book" (Lane)

IN THE VOSGES

means of a canal through the Vosges. This channel proceeds in a most romantic manner, like a silver thread running through hilly and wooded country. The waterway is now high-banked and above the level of the surrounding country, and now deep set in a rocky gorge. By repeating one feature, the picturesque rudder and stern of the barge, in various settings, I hoped to get some feeling of continuity and romantic progress on the part of this Sinbad the Sailor of a mountain pass.

In this same travel story, I found myself getting farther and farther afield until I came to a most primitive and almost medieval part of Europe, the Bohemian Forest. This was before the War, when Bohemia seemed a great deal farther away than it is to-day. I thought I had walked into a fairy tale, for the people of this land all firmly believed in witches, werwolves and vampires. I got quite used to the good folk in a village making a protective sign against the evil eye as I sketched quite inocently in their streets.

For these reasons I made most of my drawings look like the scenes in Hans Andersen's fairy tales, but they are true to topography for all that. This is the entrance to the town of Prachatitz, a living link with the fierce days of Ziska and of John Hus.

It would be interesting to test the soundness of my attempts at different treatment for different subjects. If you have not read this before do not go on reading ahead now but examine the sketch of Dode Church. I hope that the treatment of this subject leaves you a little curious. A funny little building, you say, standing by itself on a track that is certainly not suitable for motoring. It is unimpressive as architecture, therefore you possibly think the artist has drawn it for a purpose. I hope you do think so. If you don't my sketch—in one way at least—is a failure.

Now Dode Church—plain little hut as it appears—is one of the most interesting things that the romantically inclined rambler can come across. It marks a vanished village, a place literally wiped out by the Black Death. This was a prosperous place in the vineyard country of medieval England in the brave days when Rochester *exported wine to France*!

It would be useless to try and express any of this hidden romance by doing a magnificent drawing of this Norman-built village church (fallen into ruin and recently restored), because the building itself is ugly. It has a new roof and does not look at all impressive. The only hope here is to show the position of this lone relic of the lost village at the foot of the once vine-clad slope on a road that has degenerated into a mere track in the woods. You can indeed pass this little church without seeing it in the trees.

It has been my experience that the way to success in a topographical drawing is found by an enthusiastic interest in your subject. The more you know about the history of a place, the more you are interested in the people who have been there before you, the better you will be able to see its possibilities.

In this case, when I came upon Dode (which by the way is near

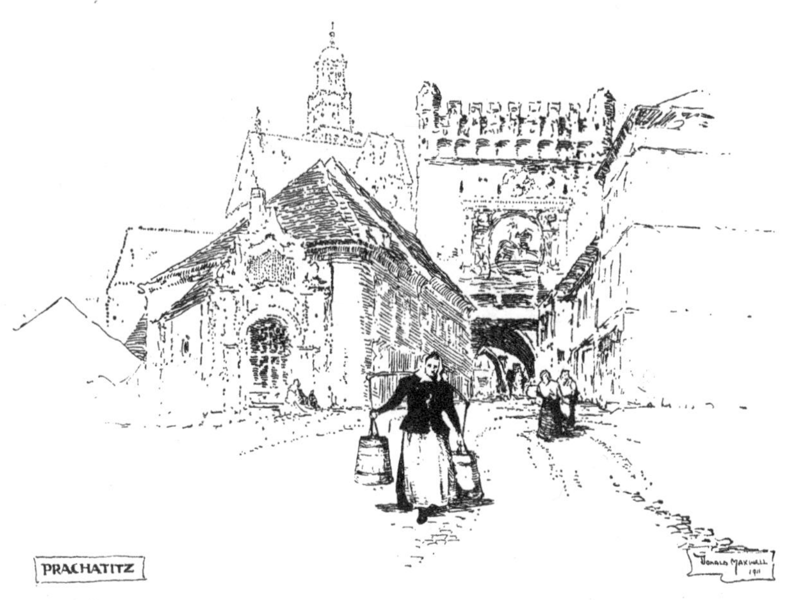

From "Adventures with a Sketch-book" (Lane)

A "Fairy-tale Town" in the Bohemian Forest

Luddesdown, which is near Rochester) I was tracking down the evidences of vineyards in the Middle Ages, and it gave me a peculiar pleasure to note the likeness of this little valley of Dode to many a scene by the banks of the gentle Moselle.

If an artist can draw at all, the stimulus of such "associative

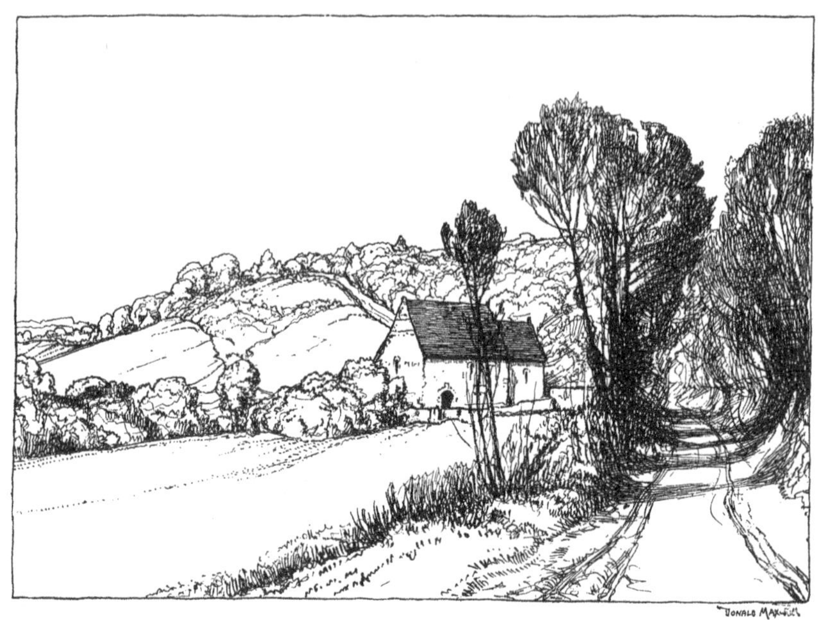

From "History with a Sketch-book" (Lane)

DODE CHURCH

excitement" will prevent him from doing a very bad picture. He is too much in sympathy with every line of the subject to fail entirely in his interpretation.

Not very long before Thomas Hardy died, I was at work on my book *Unknown Dorset*, and I had the good fortune to have some talks with the great novelist of Wessex on the subject of landscape. The upshot of our pleasant meetings was that I decided—and I could be sure of his goodwill—to compile a work on the topographical atmosphere of the great West Country classics by this author. This was done in *The Landscape of Thomas Hardy*.

Thus, I knew the Hardy country well, but when an editor asked me to draw Stinsford Church, the place where the heart of Thomas Hardy was buried, I was somewhat at a loss to make such a subject eloquent of "Under the Greenwood Tree," in which it figures under the disguise of Mellstock. All the photographs and sketches that had been published showed a picturesque old country church that might be almost anywhere.

I went down to Dorchester and one sunny morning walked to Stinsford by means of a path along by the stream. I was determined to get a good sketch of the church, but it would have to be one also that looked like a place set in woodland country, in fact, under the Greenwood Tree. Without doing any violence to the facts of the case, and by wandering awhile up and down the banks of the many-branched stream, I succeeded in getting a glimpse of the Church framed in trees, as you see here, and a picture that to some extent justified the title "Under the Greenwood Tree, the place where Thomas Hardy's heart lies buried."

Some two years ago I was asked to lecture to the art students of Gravesend. It was on the occasion of an exhibition of summer sketches and most of the work was of a very high standard. There was a tendency, however, in the case of some sketches to adopt a

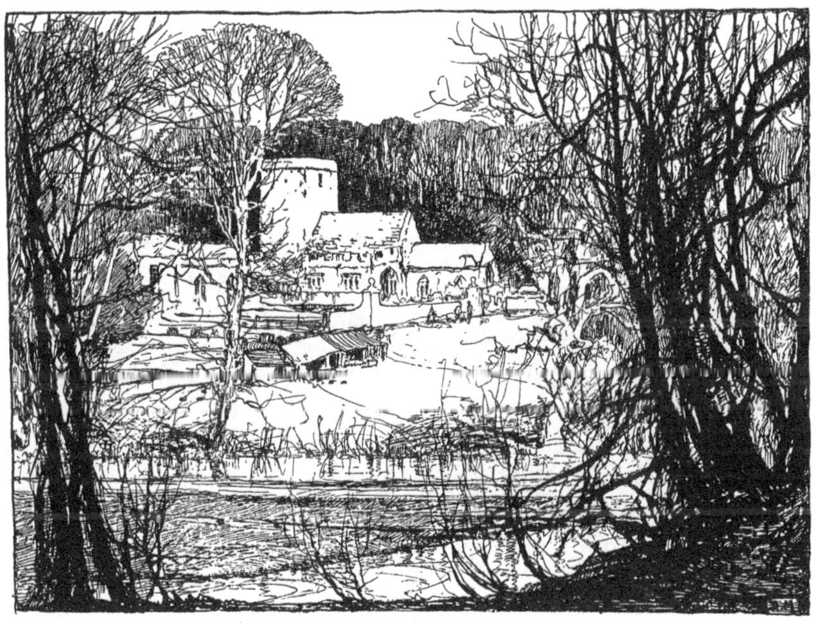

From "The Landscape of Thomas Hardy" (Cassell)

STINSFORD

technical method, in itself good, and then apply it rather indiscriminately to different subjects.

I took therefore as my theme that it was necessary for all sketchers to be detectives. A Sherlock Holmes or a Dr. Thorndyke, would look at various men and women passing by and tell you in most cases with unerring skill what trades or professions they followed. This was done by knowledge rather than mere observation. *The detective knew what to look for.* The cobbler, the typist, the motor mechanic, the doctor, the shop-walker—all had marks or mannerisms that showed their calling.

I took an example in an average landscape and asked a lot of searching questions about it. That wind-blown tree. Why was it full-domed on one side and mean and straight on the other? Because there had once been two trees and one had come down.

How long ago?

By the fact that the straight side was well grown and bushy, probably some five or six years ago.

What is the prevailing wind?

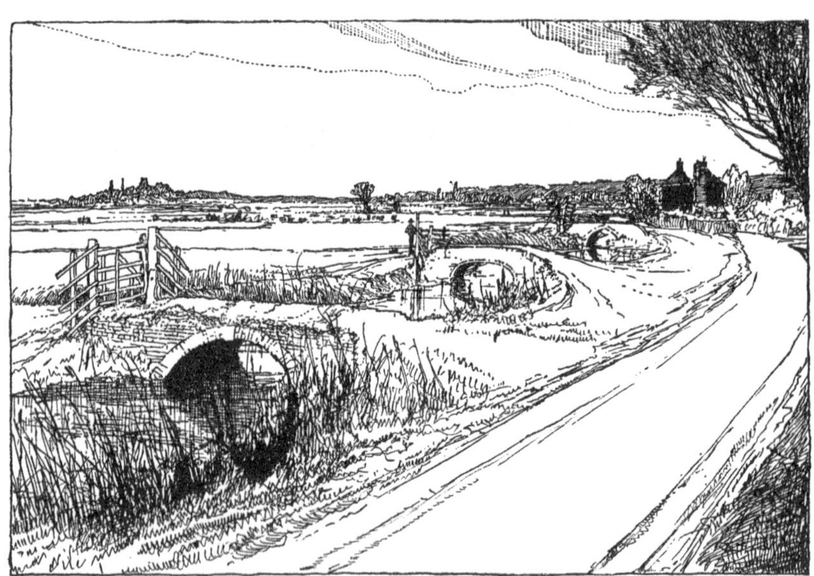

From "A Detective in Kent" (Lane)

NORTH STREAM, RECULVER

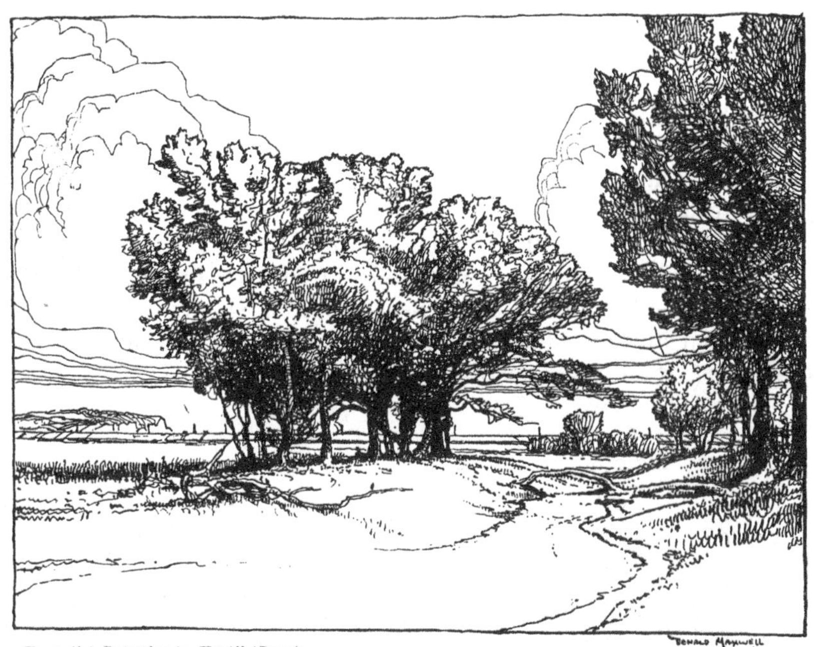

From "A Detective in Kent" (Lane)

EBBSFLEET

Where lies the sea?

Was it blown down by accident or cut down for profit?

You may not, I said, be able to answer all these questions, but by the time you have asked yourself all these, you will know something about that tree, and you will not be able to draw it unintelligently.

When I had finished, a gentleman in the audience rose to propose a vote of thanks. There was considerable amusement and not a little applause and cries of "Thorndyke!" Evidently some joke that was lost upon me.

The plot was soon out. The speaker was Dr. Austin Freeman, the famous creator of Dr. Thorndyke. He warmly commended my use of detective methods in landscape drawing.

Some time after this I developed the subject and sought to make some scientific study of method in landscape observation and deduction. The result was my book, *A Detective in Kent,* which has since been followed by *A Detective in Sussex.*

In the first of these studies I tried to trace the old coastline of the Wantsum, the waterway that formerly separated Thanet from the mainland of Kent, and the sketch shown on page 88 of the North Stream by Reculver is the last shrunken remnant of a great ship channel. It is now a rural Venice and little bridges cross the waterway and connect the "beach" with the marsh beyond. Keel Farm and Puddledock look across to Belle Isle and thence to Thanet at St. Nicholas at Wade.

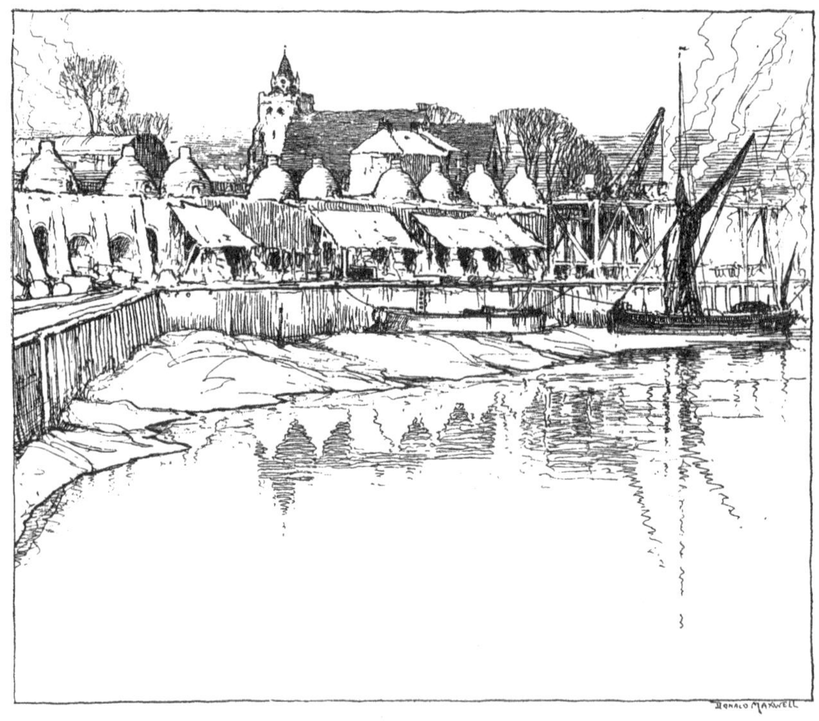

From "More Adventures among Churches" (Faith Press)

HALLING, ON THE MEDWAY

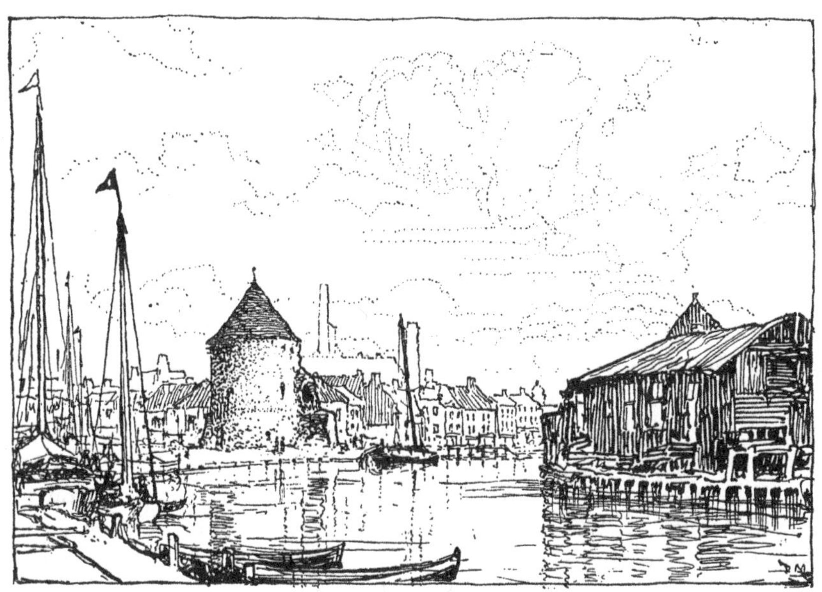

From "Unknown Norfolk" (Lane)

THE YACHT STATION, GREAT YARMOUTH

The next drawing is from the same book. It is another piece of marsh which was once seashore. Here, over thirteen hundred years ago, a small ship grounded. Out of her came strangers from Rome. They carried with them a silver cross and a picture, and they brought with them a strange story. The history of England took a new direction at this spot, so we must try and make a sketch that looks as if it is no ordinary place. Yet in itself it is a very ordinary piece of landscape, a field and a few trees.

I do not think as a matter of fact any ordinary presentment of this landscape subject could tell the story in the smallest degree, but some treatments would be better than others.

A sketch of these trees by themselves would be inadequate. They are like any others in this marsh country. However, by getting such a position that the distant sea-wall cuts across their trunks, and by showing the headland by Ramsgate, some idea of the significance of the marsh will be suggested. A keen eye will readily apprehend that there was once a time when no sea-wall existed, and when the tides made multitudinous channels through this level land.

Here, too, are three watery landscapes, each attempting to illustrate a particular character of river scenery. The first is of a village in the heart of the Medway country a few miles above Rochester. It lies in the Land of Cement, and this land has to me, and I think to many, a peculiar likeness here and there to the East. The drift of cement dust falls on everything, and is then fixed by dew and rain so that many buildings are incrusted in a covering of pale honey-coloured material often several inches thick. This blunts the corners of walls, windows and buildings, and gives them the appearance of ancient sun-baked walls, and in sunny lights often gives them an Arabian Nights glamour that is both curious and pleasing. At Halling is a row of old bottle-kilns that might be domes of mosques.

The second of these river sketches is of the yacht station at Great Yarmouth. This is the main starting place for the yachts and wherries that are to go up and explore the watery world of the broads. The treatment is intended to be an overture to the breezy landscape that is to come, a flat expanse of smooth waters, level plains of green fields, and great skies of marching clouds.

The third of these subjects, however, is in Langport, which is on the great plain of Sedgmoor, that one-time inland sea of Somerset.

It is drained now and some of it presents features not unlike those seen in Holland and Flanders.

The "rhines" and channels intersect the pasture everywhere and there are sluggish waters in Langport, one of which I have drawn here, which might be found in Bruges or Ypres.

And now for some problems of treatment and interpretation in drawing buildings. Not long ago an editor sent me off to draw some Cathedrals and two of these are contrasted on pages 86 and 87 respectively.

There are many treatments possible. I chose one that would make Ely look as big and majestic as possible and Southwark as small and homely as possible, for this seemed to me to be the "note" of each as a church. Across the flat land of the Fen, the Cathedral of

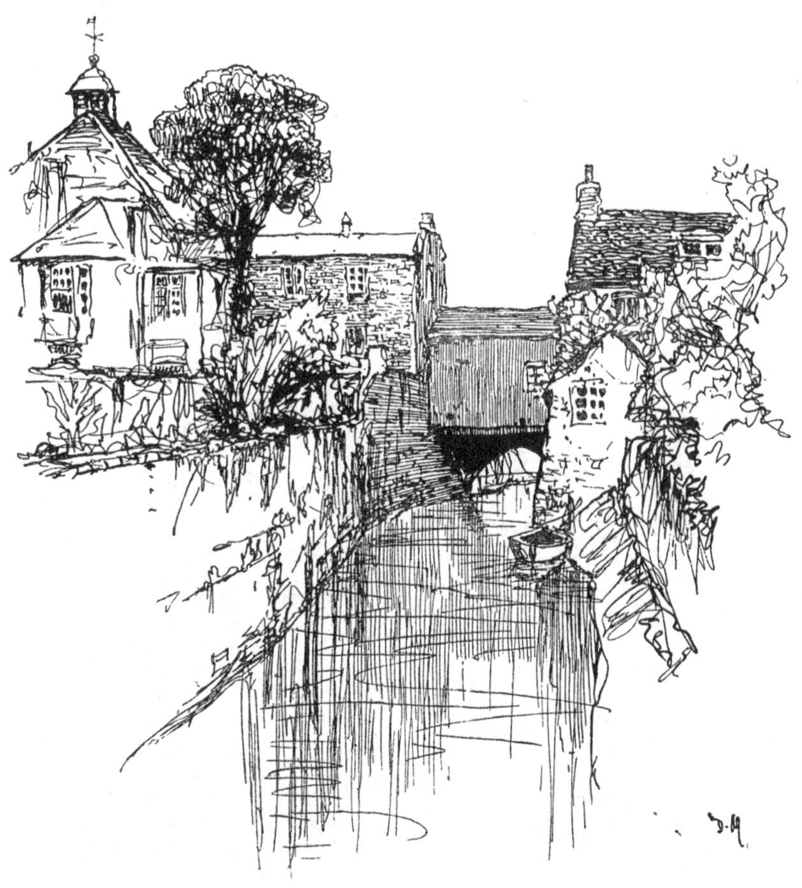

From "Unknown Somerset" (Lane)

IN LANGPORT

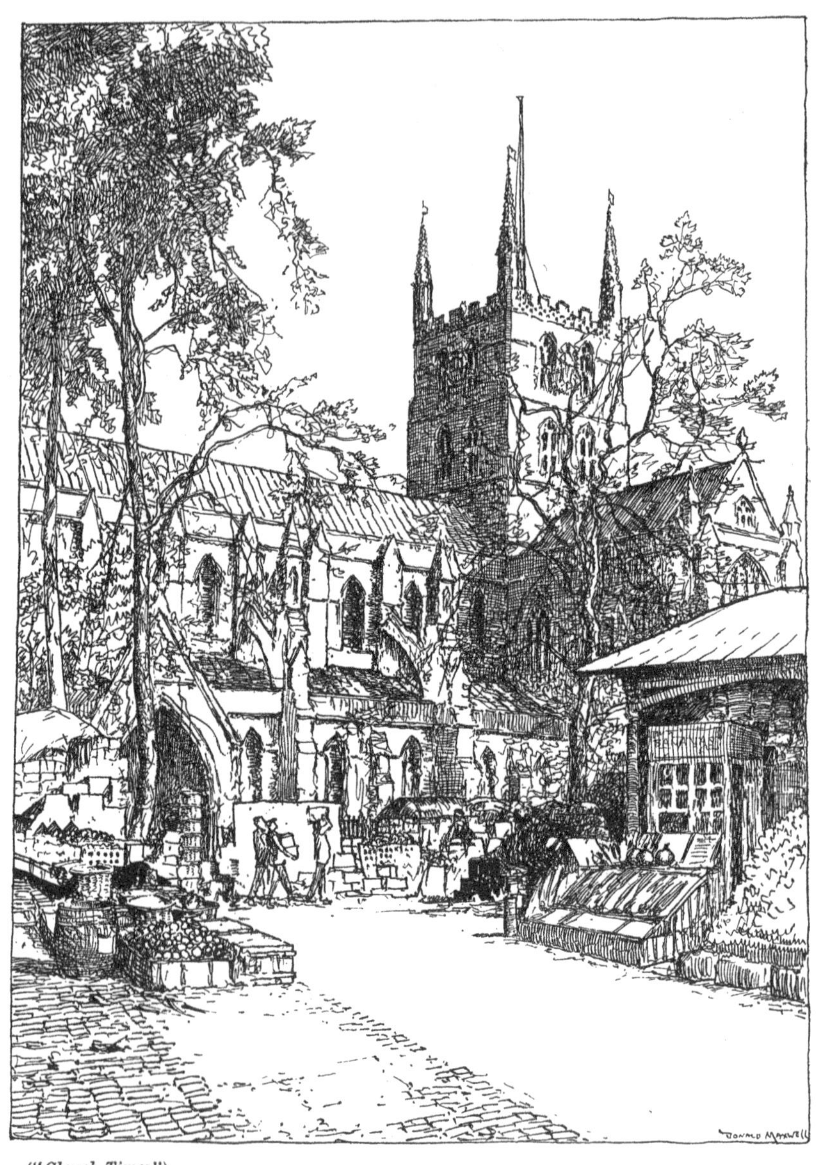

("*Church Times*")

OUR SAVIOUR OF THE MARKET, SOUTHWARK

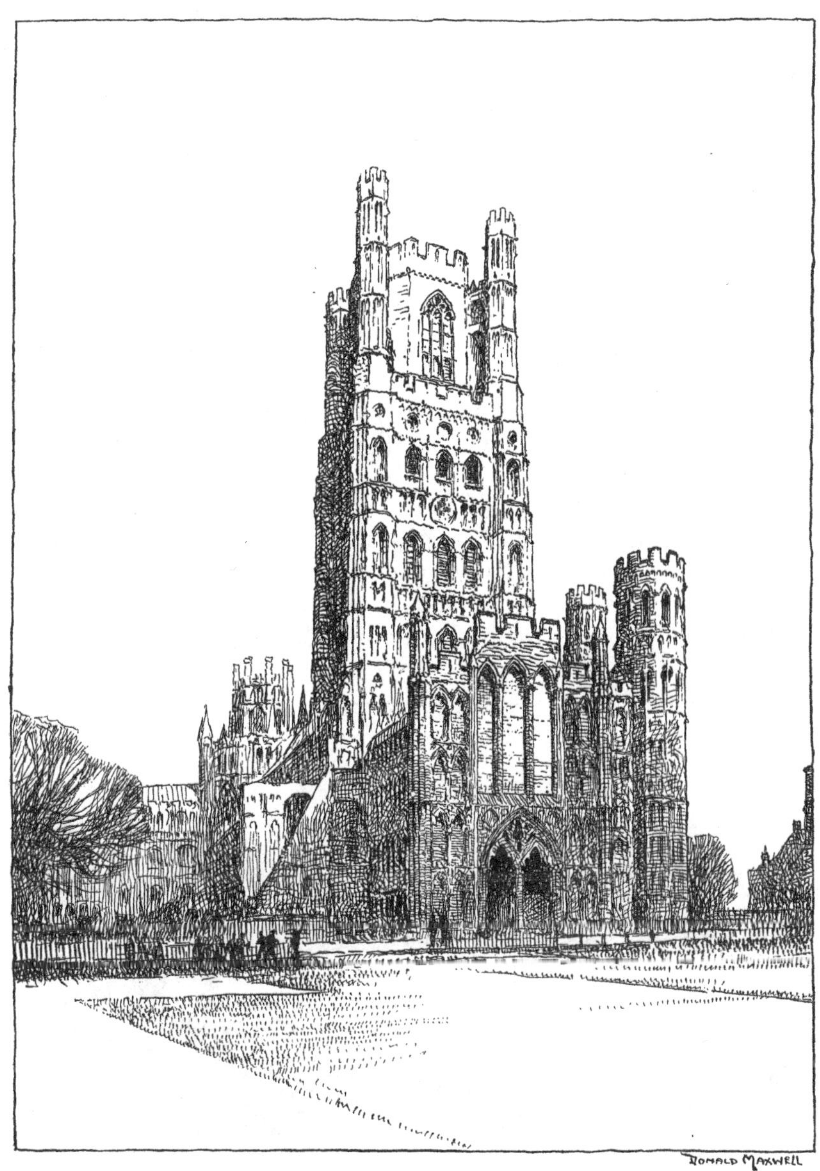

(*"Church Times"*)

ELY

Ely looks enormous. The tremendous height of it towering into the sky, is the outstanding memory of this great thing.

Now my drawing of it, here seen, is not one that would probably enthuse an architect. It is not particularly good in its detail, and many features, from an architectural draughtsman's point of view, are ill-drawn. It was the best thing I could do in the time, however, and although it lacks much, I think it does express height. This is done by a simple artifice, by keeping the detail work lighter at the top and somewhat heavier and more toned as it comes lower and lower down.

Southwark, however, could not possibly be made to look overpowering and majestic. It is built in a hidden way in such manner that it can be seen only in bits. It is all mixed up with the Market, which overflows the precincts of St. Saviour's and hems it in with cabbages and sacks.

But it is a friendly and homely corner of Old Southwark. We have not much time for attending services in the early morning. We are all rushing about with baskets and boxes, but we like to see the buttresses of the old church, through avenues of fruit, and its bells have a restful sound, and our children go to the children's

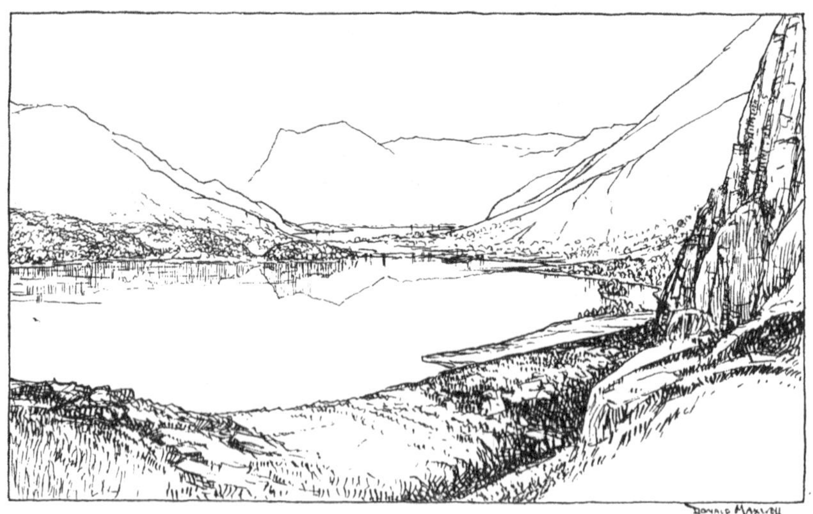

(Cavendish)

CRUMMOCK WATER

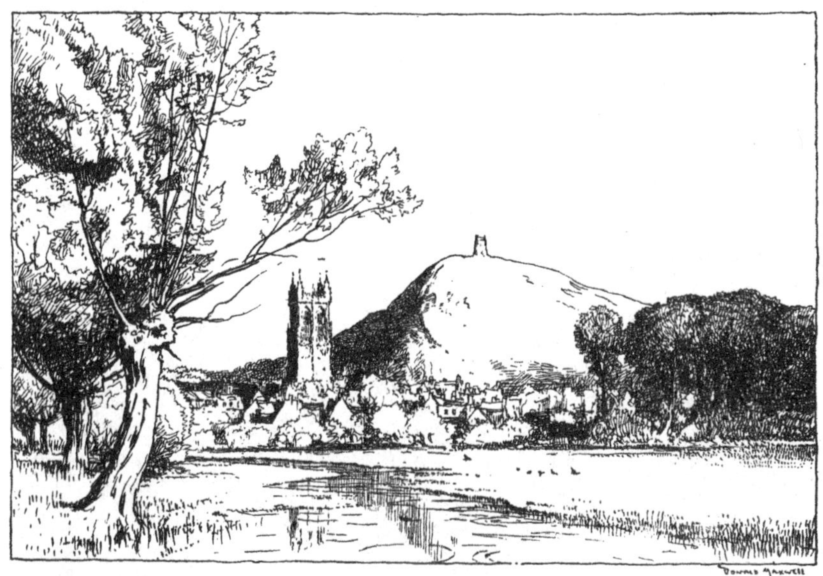

("*Church Times*")

GLASTONBURY

service in the afternoon. To work is to pray, and so we get through a lot of praying outside, and besides, if ever we do have our solemn thoughts about religion, it is to St. Saviour's we turn. And so I thought I would draw it as on page 86, and called the picture "Our Saviour of the Market."

The next two pictures are attempts—I hope in some measure successful—to give an atmosphere of reality to two very different subjects.

The one in the Lake District owes any merit it has to the *exact* reflection of the mass of the distant mountain in the water—by its absolute stillness telling of a mountain lake and nothing else—and the other is of Glastonbury, a place of legend and romance.

All these subjects are such that they can be treated without much tone, but there are others, as the one of Thaxted Church, that demand large surfaces of shading. This is not difficult, but it takes a tremendous time. A series of drawings with as much tone in them as this one would take four or five times as long to work out as those which we have been considering.

A portion of "Burlingham" grey paper, reproduced the exact size of original. It should be further reduced to size of block on page 94.

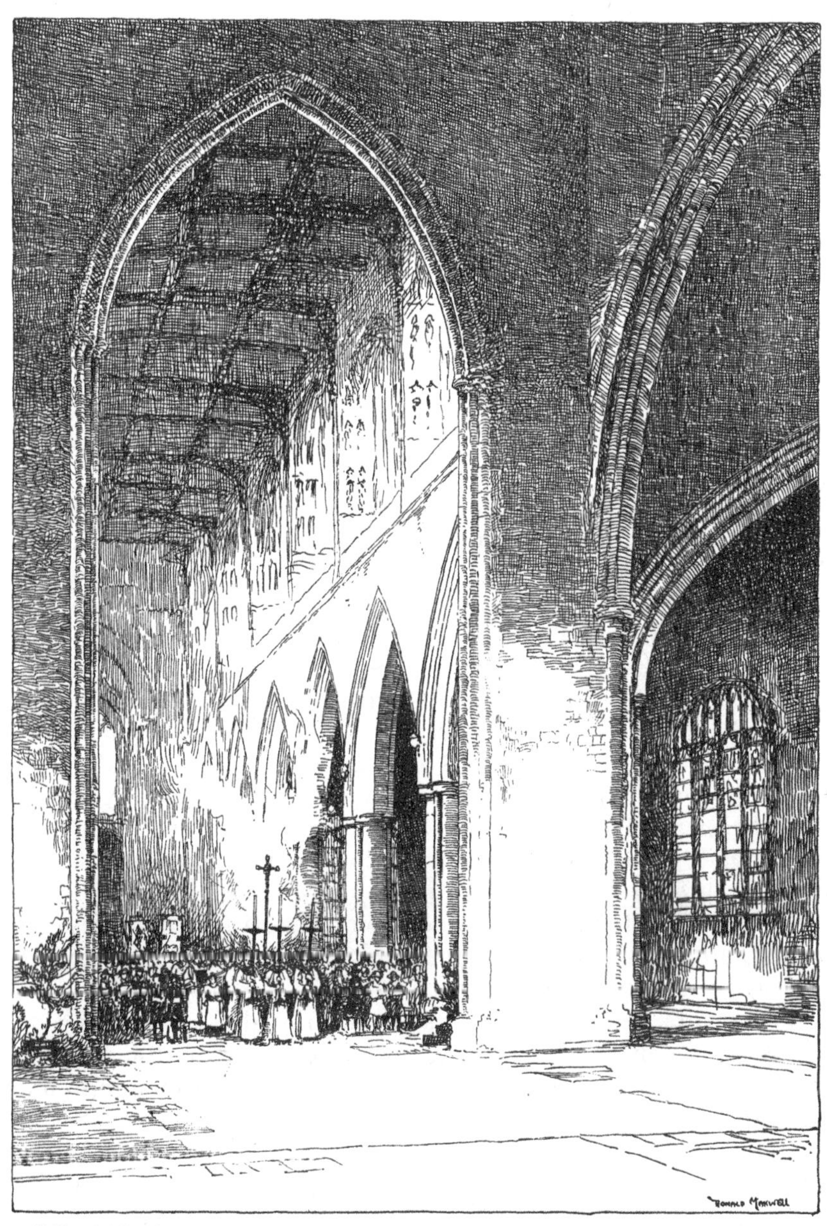

("*Church Times*")

A TRINITY PROCESSION IN THAXTED CHURCH

In the case of night scenes and effects of looming mist or dark masses of foliage, the problem is well nigh insoluble—except with a great amount of time in hand—and this is the one thing the traveller or press correspondent will not have.

The temptation to use an ordinary engraver's mechanical tone in places is great. I have seldom tried it in landscape because in large surfaces the effect *is* mechanical. In the hands of a clever artist there are cases in figure subjects, conventional designs, and architectural pictures where a mechanical tone can be used with good effect, but I have never known a nocturne "come off" successfully with mechanical means.

I have given an immense amount of time and thought to the problem and I have at last found a means of getting a mechanical tone that does not look mechanical.

The experiments I made seemed to be endless, but at last I found a granulation of resin that "broke up" by chemical means into a pattern so varied and so rhythmical that it gave an effect of which I had dreamed for years.

Look at the drawing opposite, a nocturne of Birmingham.

It is reproduced as an ordinary line drawing, and this block was not made from the original but from a newsaper print, which shows how successful is the black and white effect without any half-tone screen or other device to break it up. The "mesh" of the black and white is very coarse, about equivalent to a very noticeable screen if it were photographically reproduced, yet it is delicate and mobile because of the immense variety of its texture. It cannot fill up in quick printing like a half-tone block often does, because the white intervals are so large. The pattern never repeats itself, so it does not tire the eye as does any sort of woven mesh that is the same over a large area.

I venture to think that this invention will be a godsend to harassed sketchers who are working against time on tonal effects that must be produced in the text of a book and therefore in line and set with the type.

The plate on page 90 shows a fragment of "Burlingham" grey paper produced the exact size of the original. For purposes of reproduction it can be reduced a little as in examples on pages 94 and 95. The reduction most successful is from 4 to 3. Any

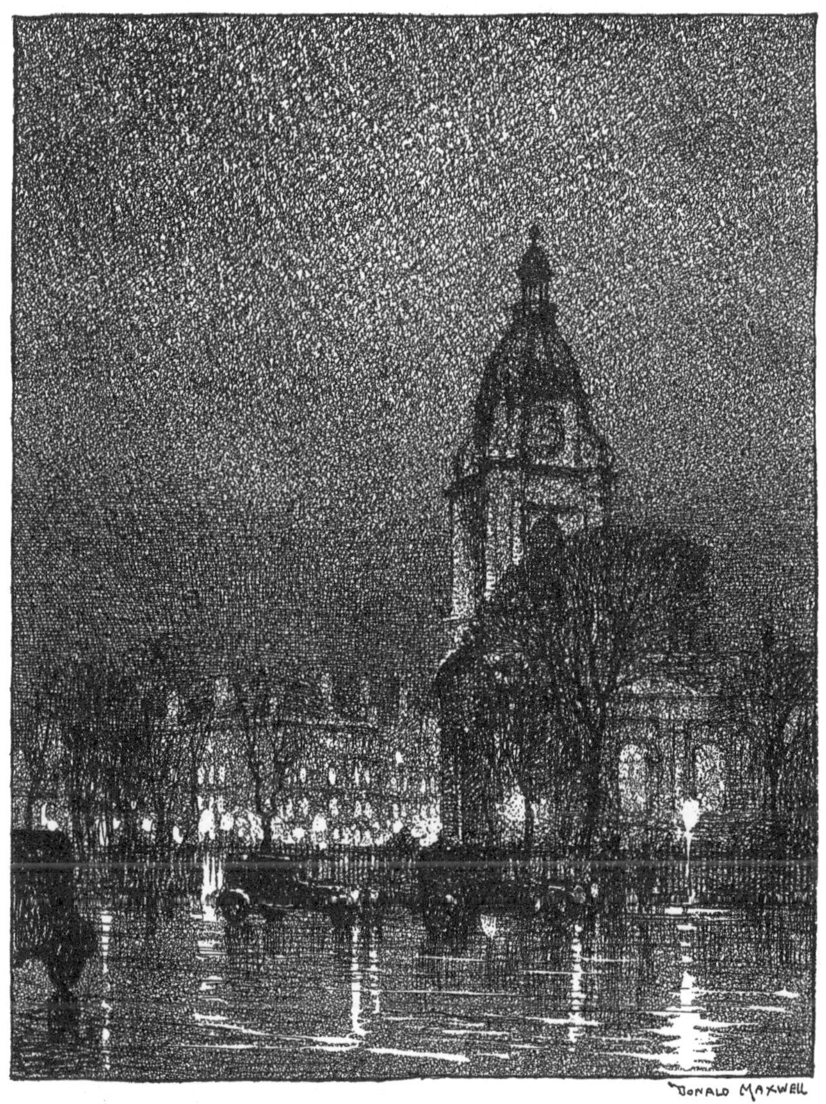

("*Church Times*")

A NOCTURNE OF BIRMINGHAM

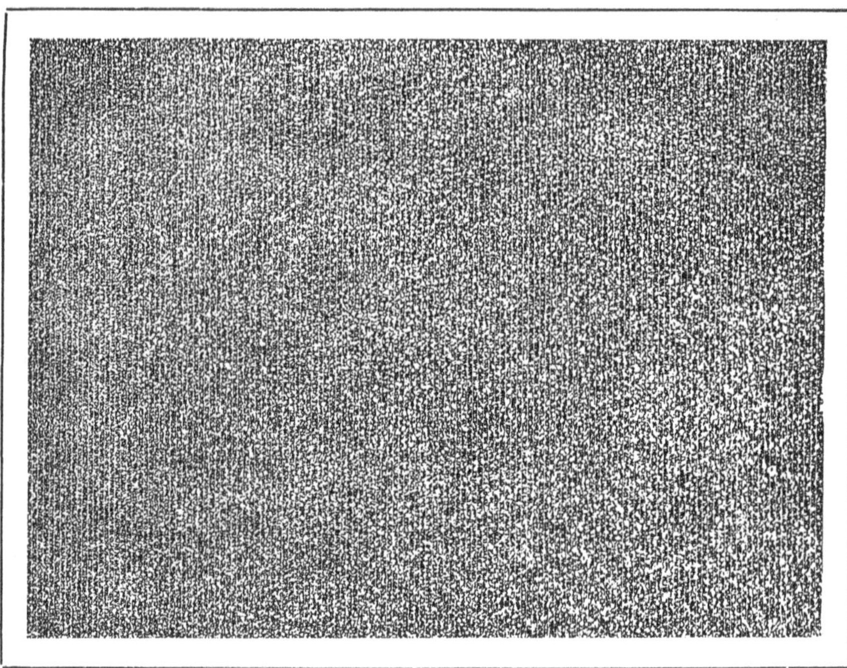

FIG. 1. "TWILIGHT"

This is a piece of "Burlingham" grey paper. It appears grey, but is made up of a varied texture of black lines of a very irregular pattern.

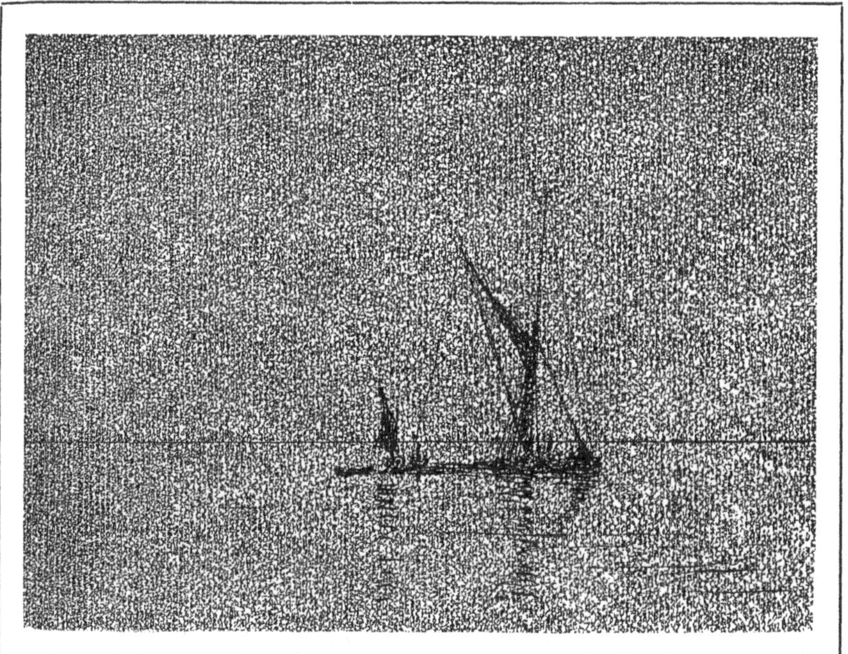

FIG. 2. "TWILIGHT"

For scenes with much tone in them this grey paper can be used to sketch on in black and white. Here is the first stage of a drawing—a barge sketched in with black ink. Nothing but the barge, its reflection, and the horizon line is indicated.

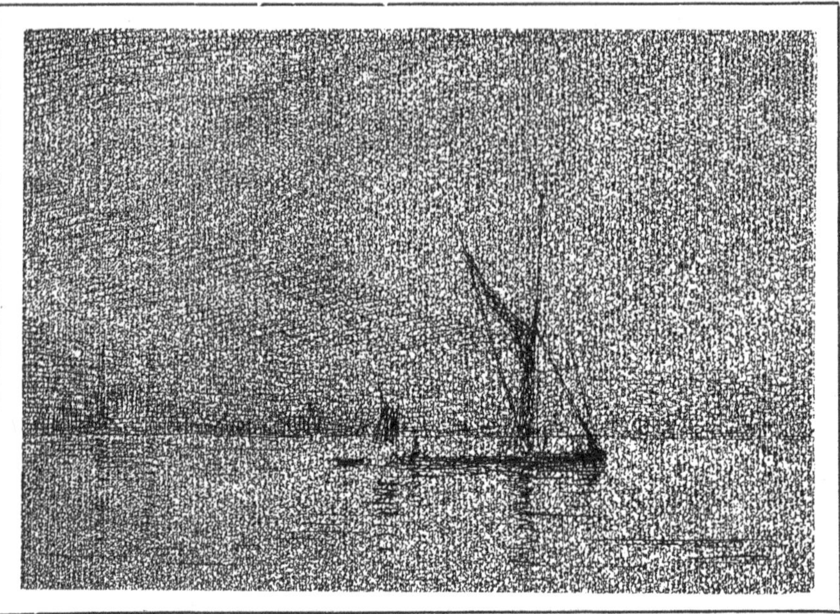

FIG. 3. "TWILIGHT"

The next stage of the sketch is the representation of the darker tones of lower sky, drawn over the grey with a fine pen.

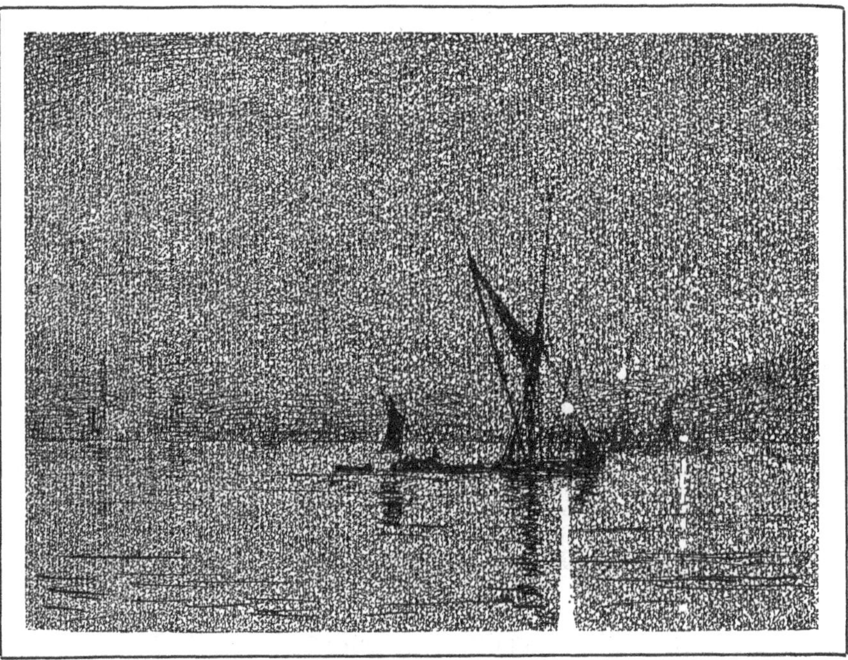

Fig. 4. "Twilight"

Now we are putting in the principal lights with a fine brush—chinese white or process white—and we have added the small steamer which is passing down the river.

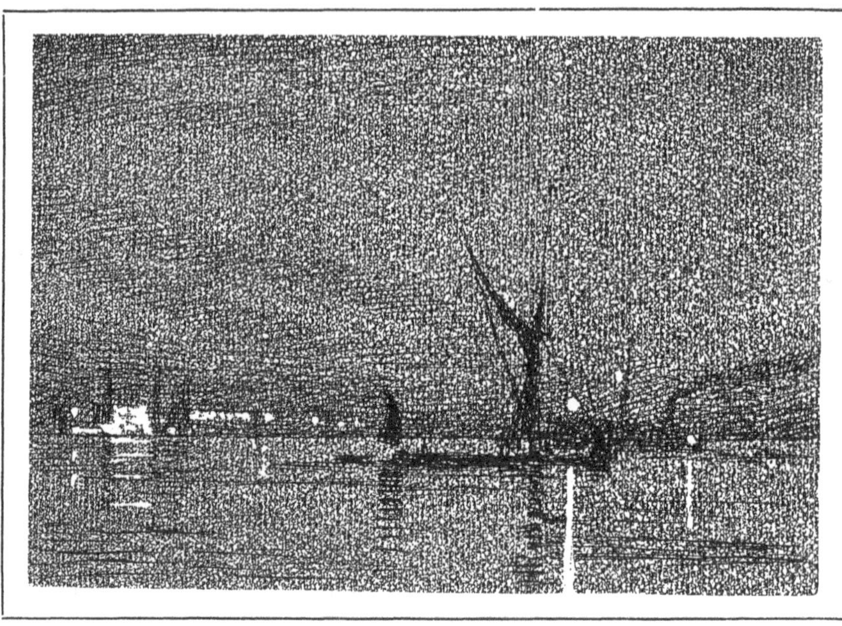

FIG. 5. "TWILIGHT"

Some cement works show lights on shore, and we indicate these in main masses

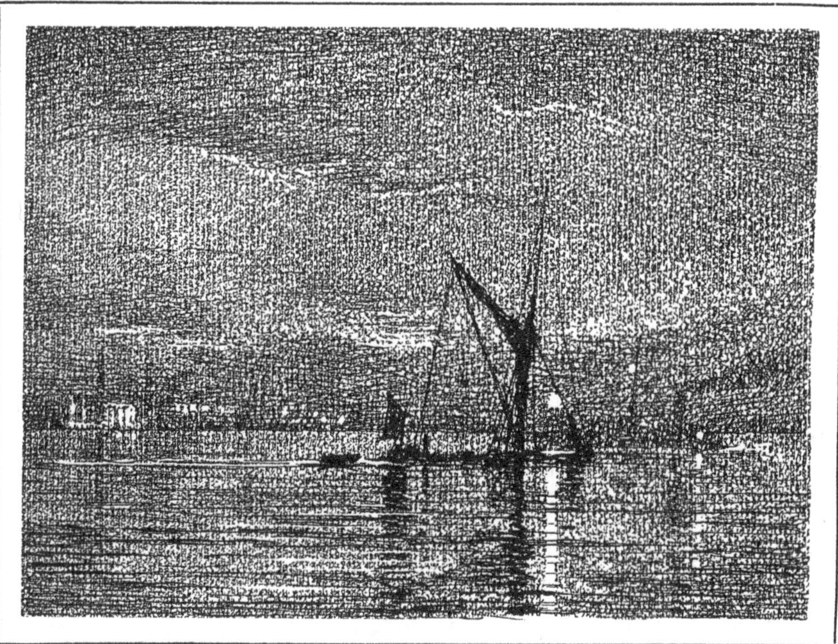

Fig. 6. "Twilight"

and then tone down these whites and give a little more light and shade to the twilight sky and its reflections in the river. This to an experienced sketcher will all take about ten minutes, but drawn in line on white paper such a picture would take hours.

greater reduction than this might fill up the smaller white flicks, and this would tend to darken and coarsen the tone.

There are so many effects of twilight, sunset, and night that take only a few minutes in wash and yet in line are interminable problems. With this paper you have practically a grey tone to work upon and you can draw on it in black ink and chinese white, and get the effect of a wash monochrome.

Let us imagine that we are in Venice and see a subject which we very much want to do, but alas, we have not much time and a wash drawing will be no good. Our Burlingham grey paper comes to the rescue.

Remember, I am supposed now to be writing for experienced sketchers. This is no medium of uncertainty and experiment, because you cannot draw in pencil without risking a mess when it comes to rubbing it out. You must put down what you want in clear, decisive strokes. Still more decisive when you come to put in strokes with chinese white, for remember, every mark on the paper must be either full black or full white. Any fumbling with chalky half-tones will be fatal.

I have reproduced three other examples of this drawing with various uses of this "Burlingham" grey paper. The first of these is a "Nocturne of Birmingham," on page 93. This is a "first edition" of my invention as far as the ground-paper is concerned. It has not got the effect of a "laid" paper that I think is more pleasing. It is without the thin white lines running through it. However, for a dark effect it does very well. The next picture—on page 94—is a twilight subject I sketched in Fiddler's Reach, near Gravesend. This is drawn on the same ground-paper as the "Nocturne of Birmingham," but an engraver's mechanical tone of white lines has been run through the sky and water to lighten the effect.

The original texture of the ground is so irregular in its blacks and whites that the mechanical tone lightens without making the ground look at all like a mechanical texture.

The third and last example is a sketch that I made myself from a group in my large altar-piece in the Garrison Church, Chatham. The ground on which this black-and-white panel is drawn is really a paper mosaic. Before I started the sketch I stuck white paper

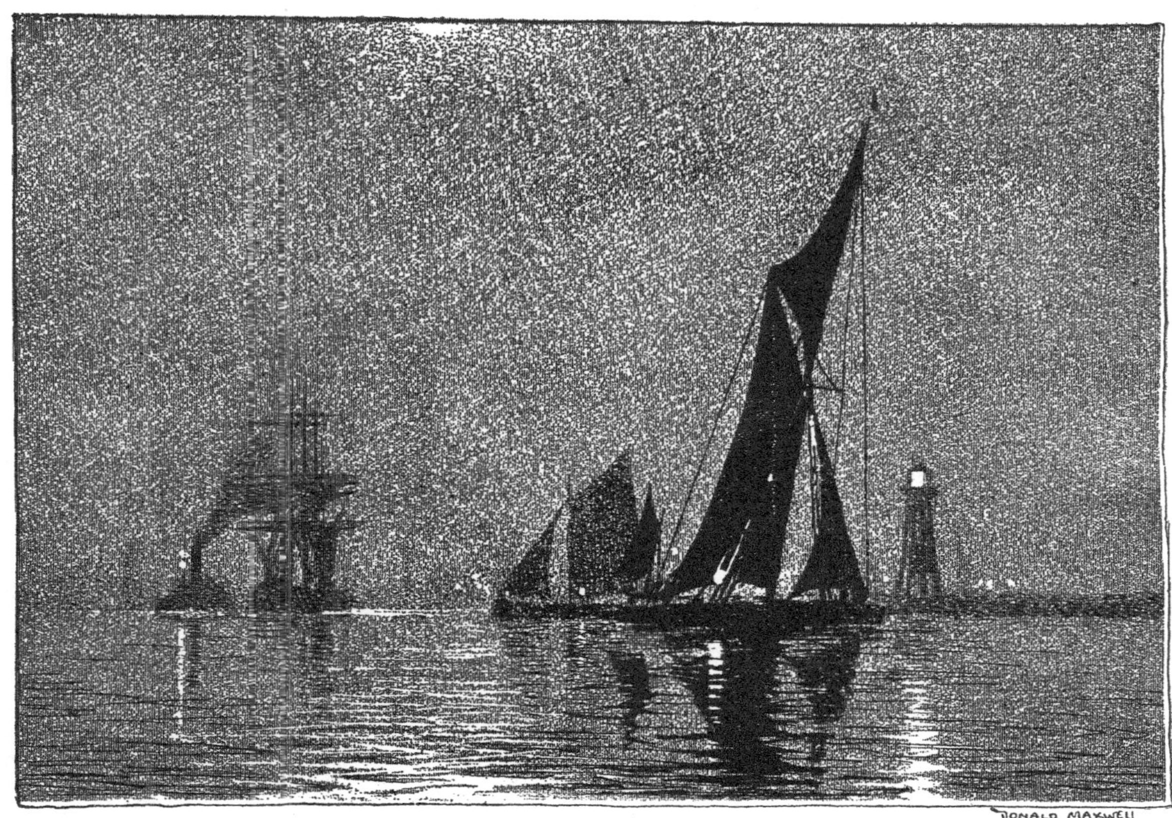

(*Cavendish*) DONALD MAXWELL

FIDDLER'S REACH

in the centre and "Burlingham" grey paper on the sky edges and foreground. Thus, although a perfectly workmanlike surface on which to build up an elaborate pen drawing, the ground is varied. Where there is a great deal of white needed, the white ground is better than the grey, but for deep tonal passages this "Burlingham" grey gives a rich quality to the pen work and the device saves an enormous amount of time.

I think you will agree that the effect is as rich in its varying greys as a wash drawing, and has the advantage of being reproducible on the cheapest and flimsiest paper as on a heavy "art" surface, and has, moreover, the enormous advantage over a half-tone inasmuch as it can be printed with the type.

With these few hints to beginners, advice to fellow-workers, and greetings of love and respect to living masters of line—of which some account is given in Part V—I must here leave the subject and the problems of sketching in pen and ink.

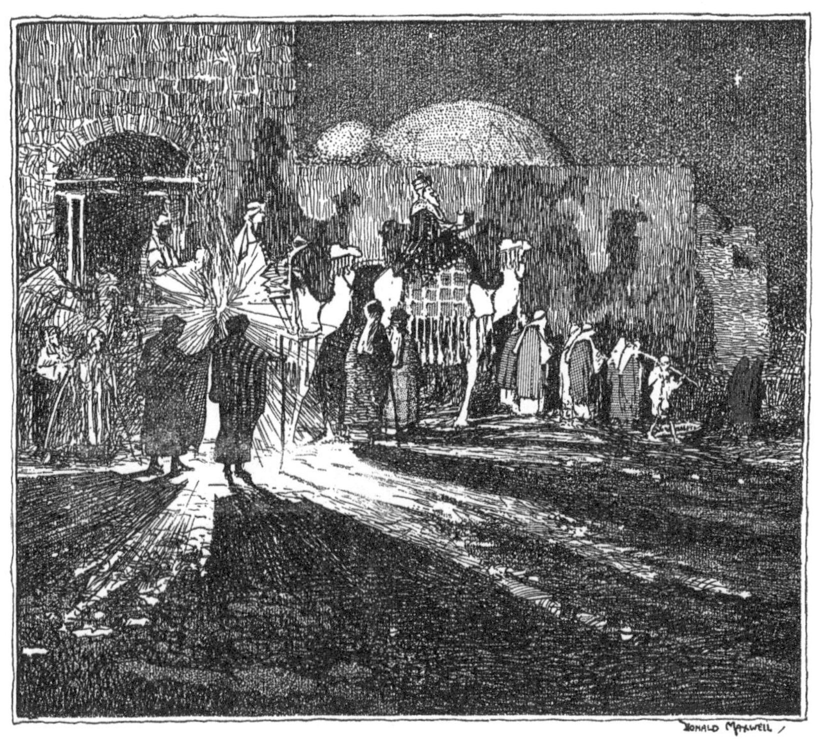

(*Cavendish*)

THE WISE MEN

PART V

A GALLERY OF CONTEMPORARY PEN AND INK LANDSCAPES

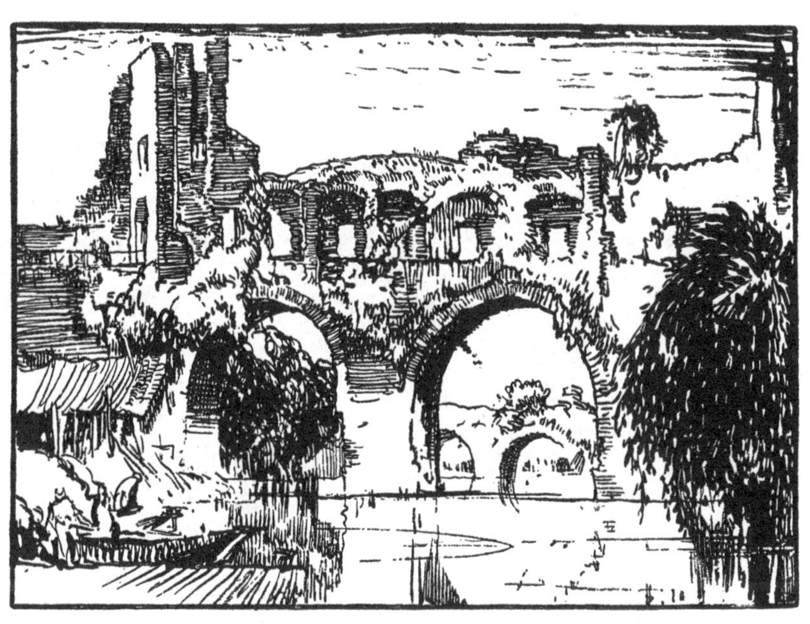

Illustration by Frank Brangwyn, "At Zutphen in Holland," from *A Book of Bridges* (Lane)

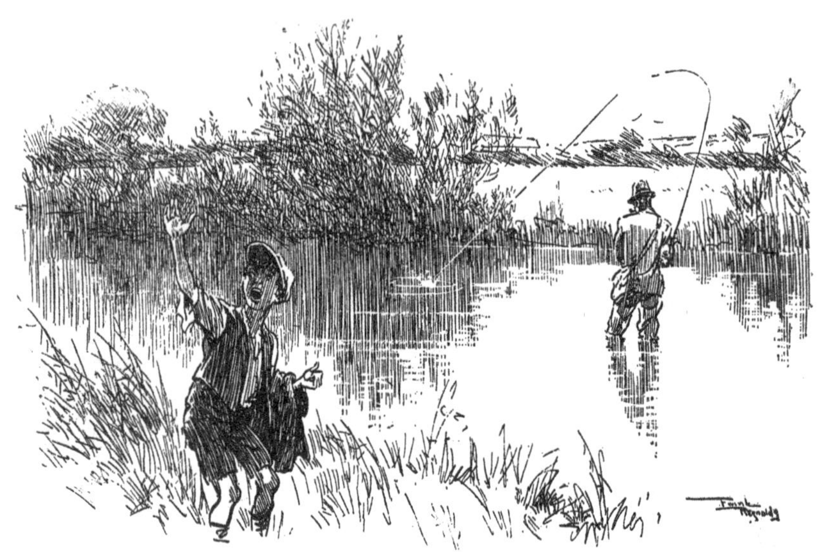

Illustration by Frank Reynolds, from *Punch*

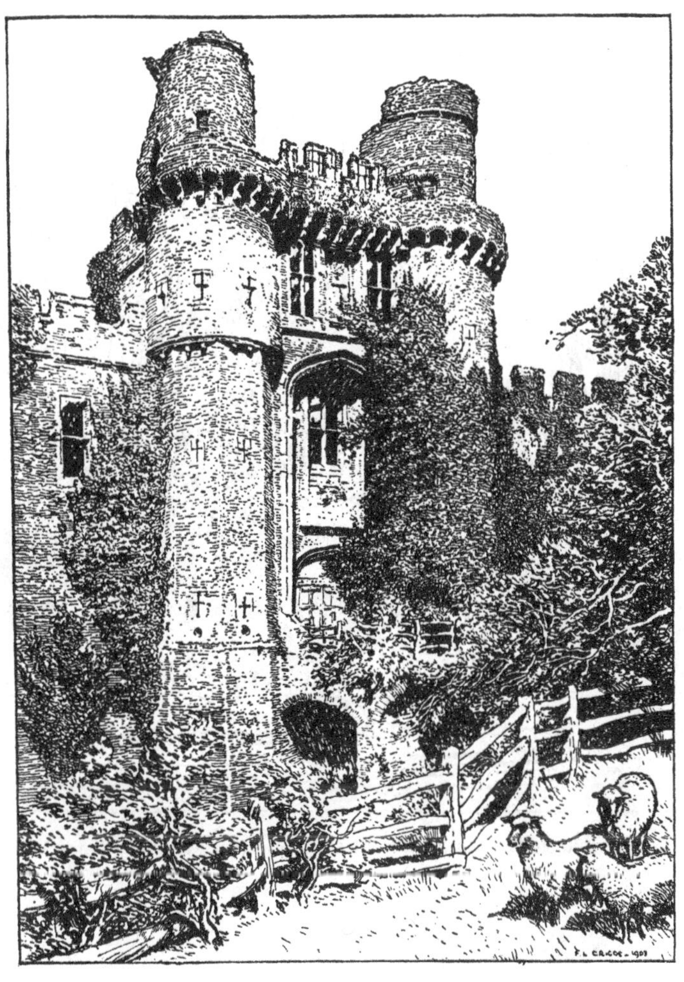

Illustration by F. L. Griggs, "Hurstmonceux Castle," from *Highways and Byways in Sussex* (Macmillan)

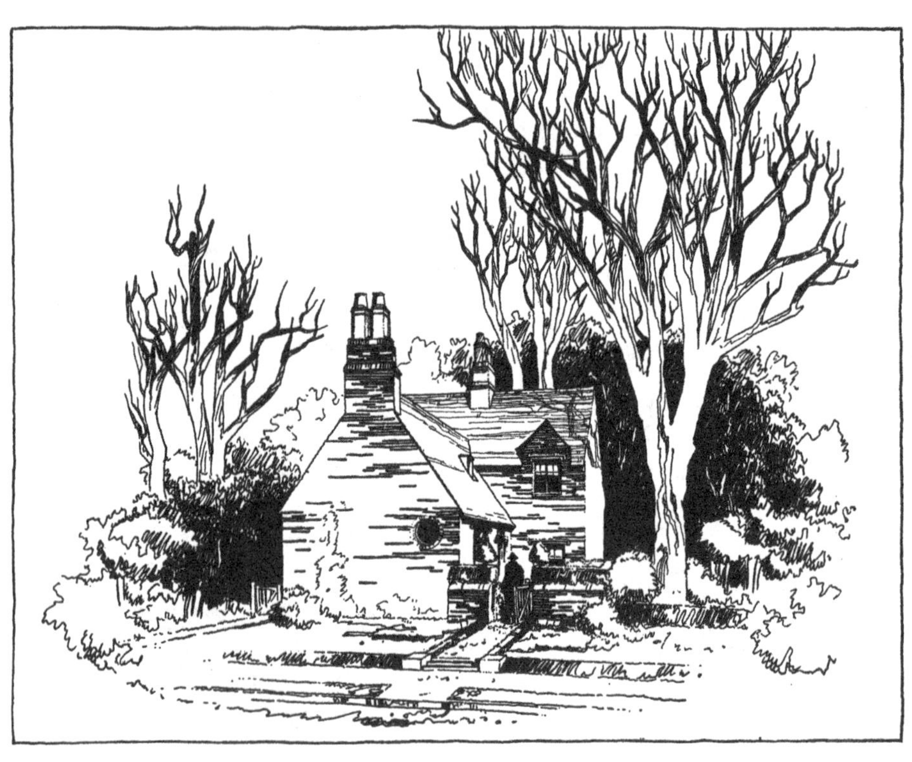

Design for a Five-Room House by Angus McD. McSweeney, Architect (San Francisco, CA)

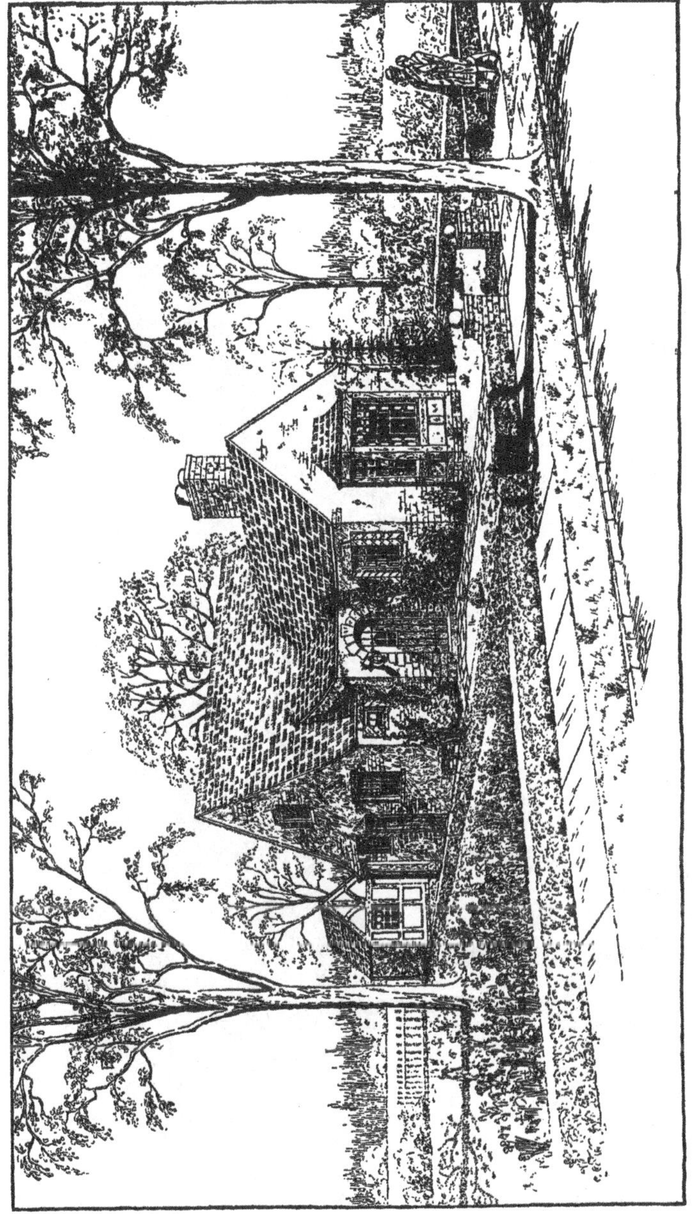

Design for a Five-Room House by Clyde E. Light, Architect (Detroit, MI)

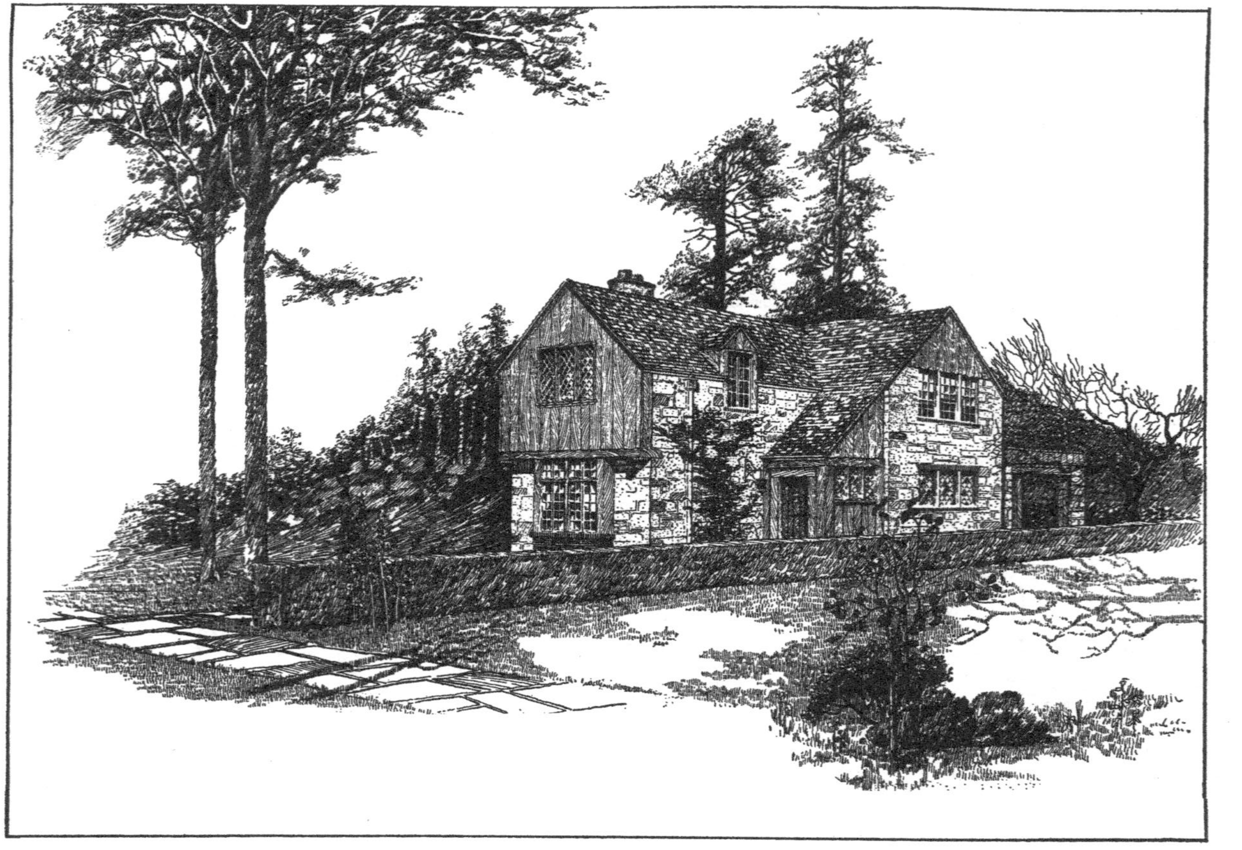

Design for a Five-Room House by Charles A. Markley, Architect (Utica, NY)

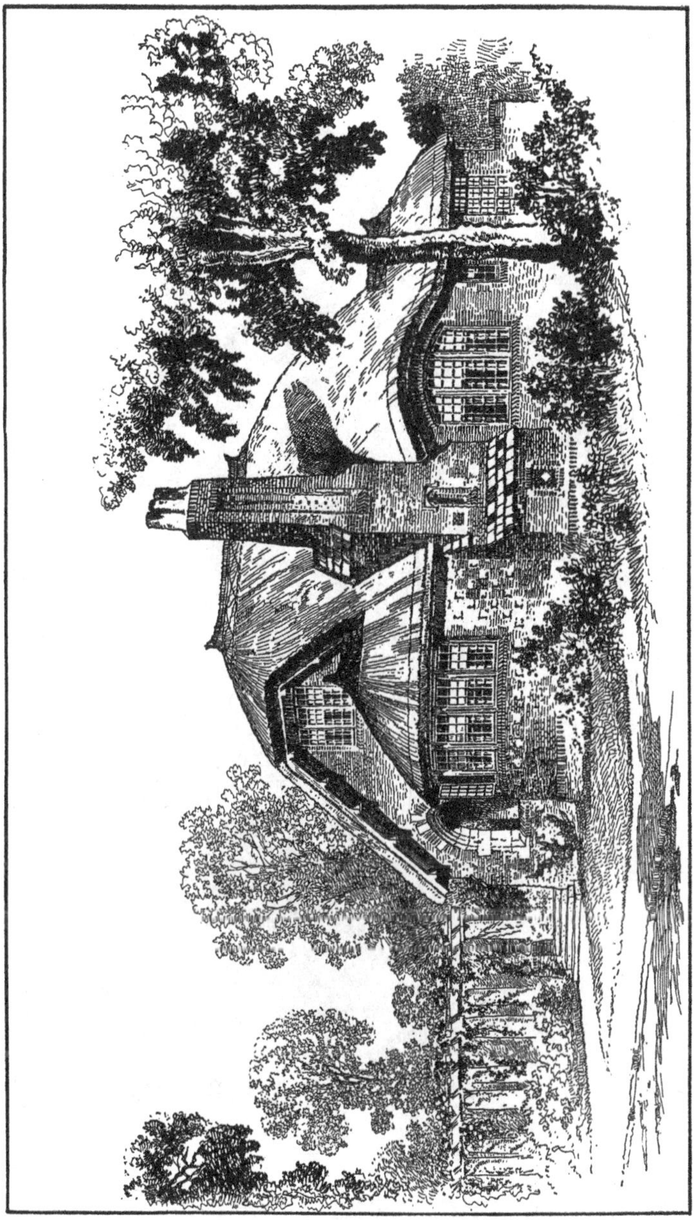

Design by Hubert G. Ripley, Architect (Boston, MA)

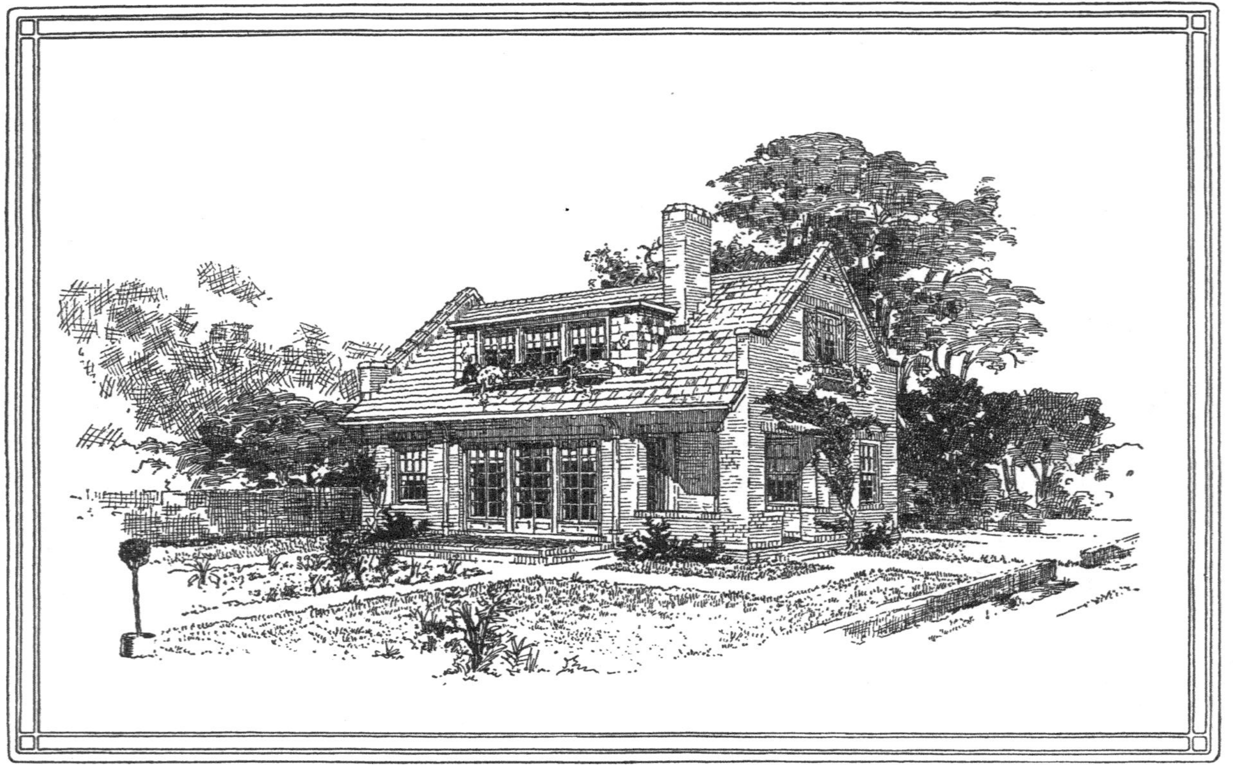

Design by William R. Schmitt, Architect (New York, NY)

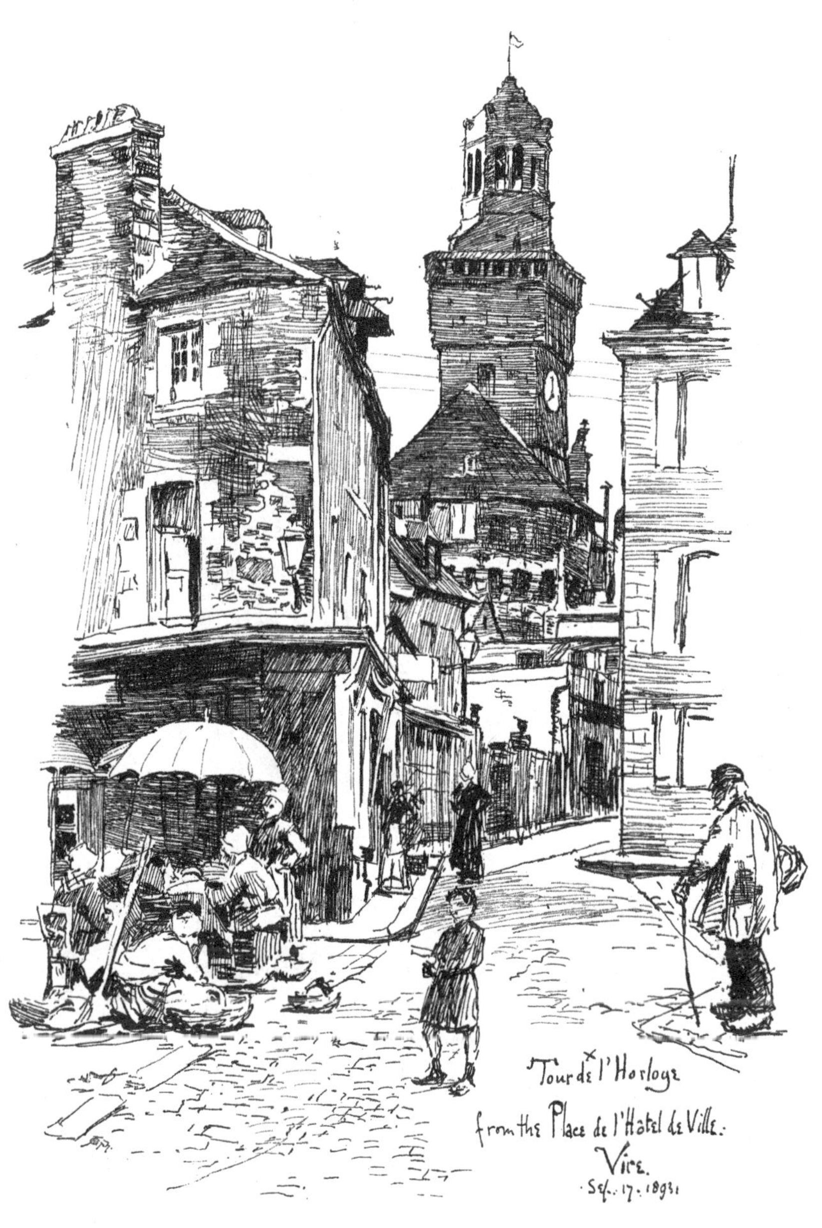

Illustration by Bernard Partridge, "Tour de l'Horloge, Vire"

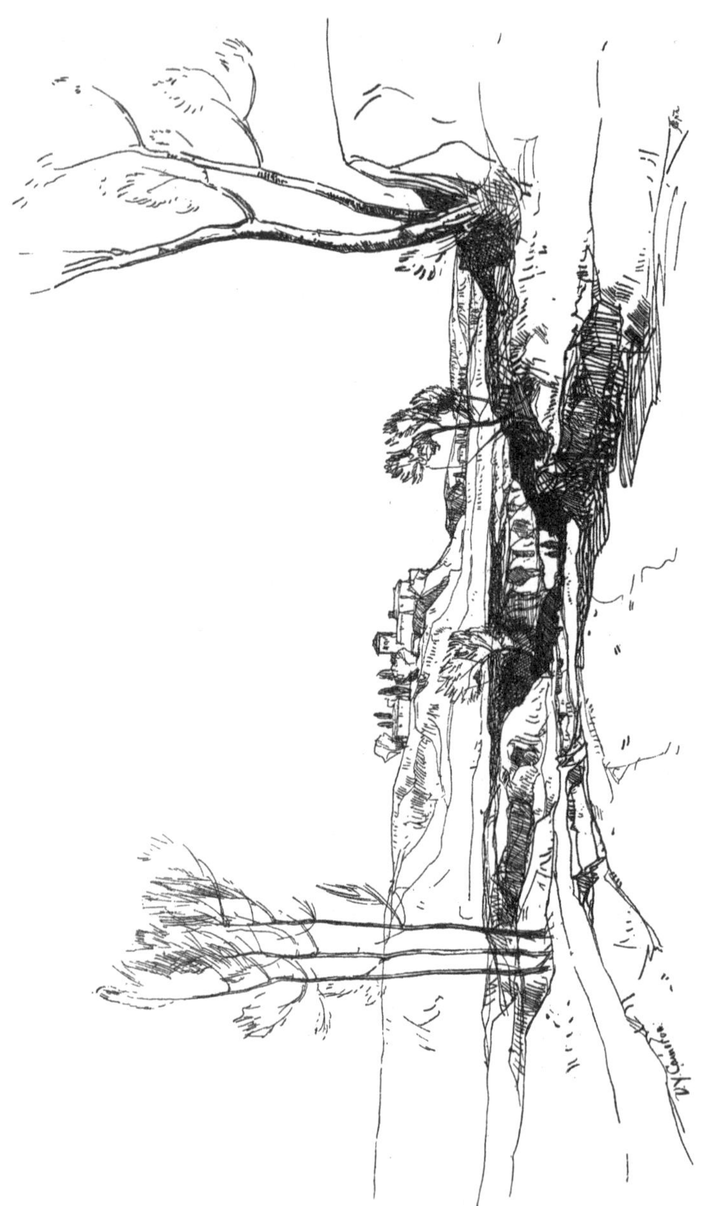

Illustration by D. Y. Cameron, "A Road in Tuscany"

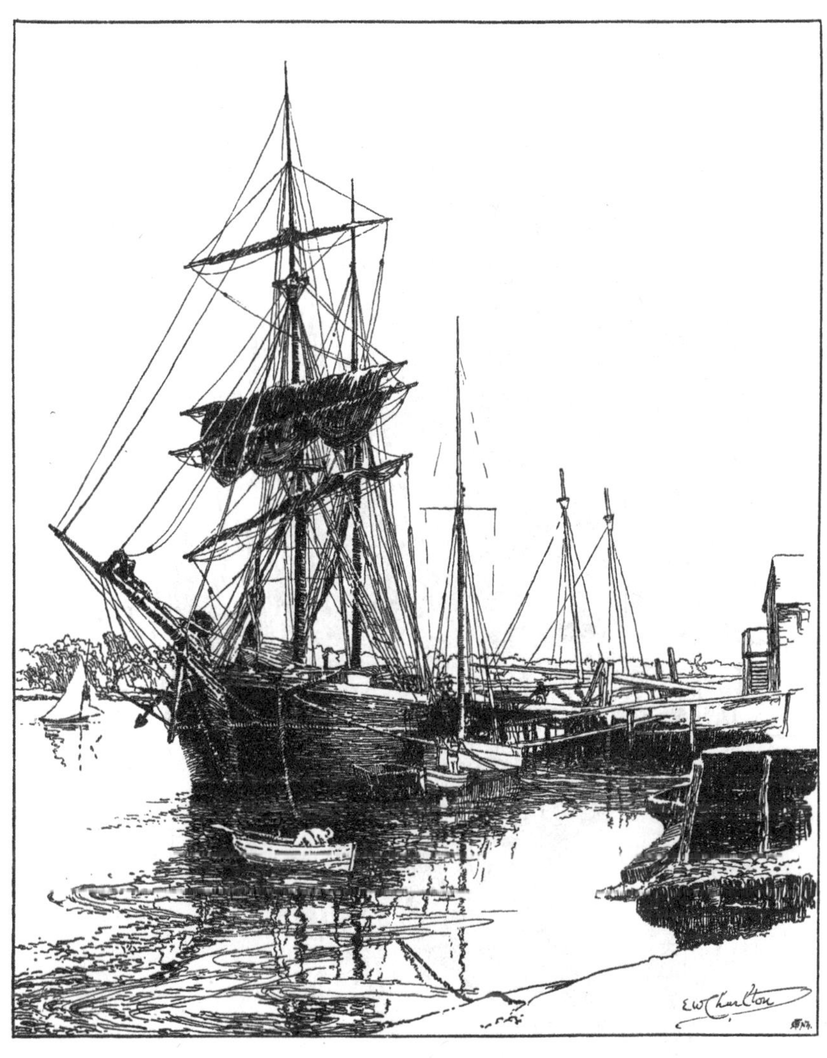

Illustration by E. W. Charlton, "On the Quay, Lymington"

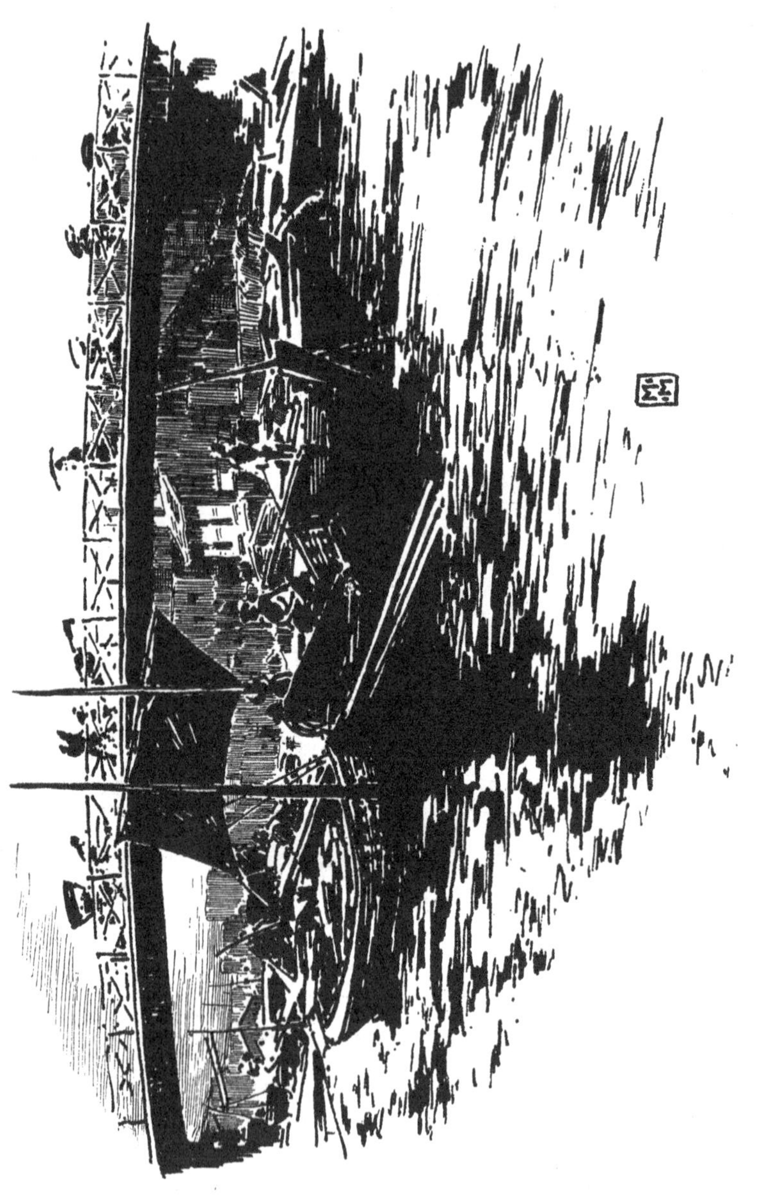

Illustration by Mortimer Menpes, "Osaka, Japan"

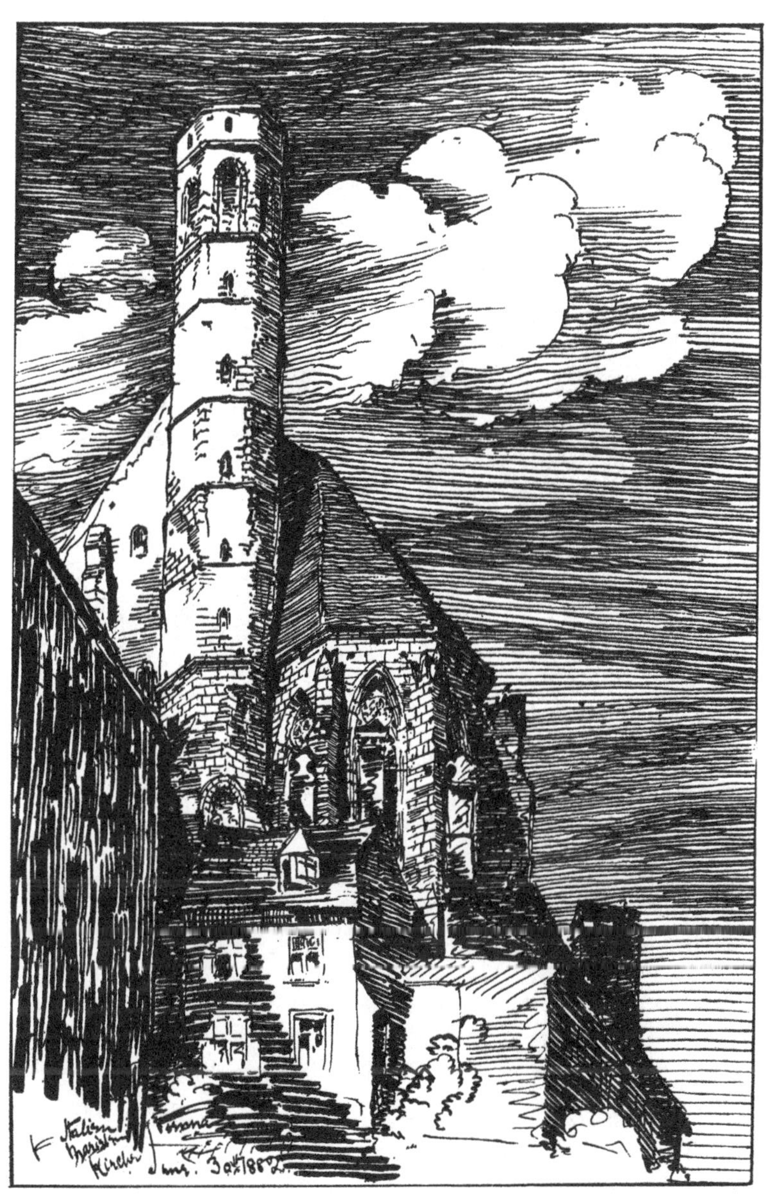

Illustration by Beresford Pite, "The Italian Marienkirche, Vienna"

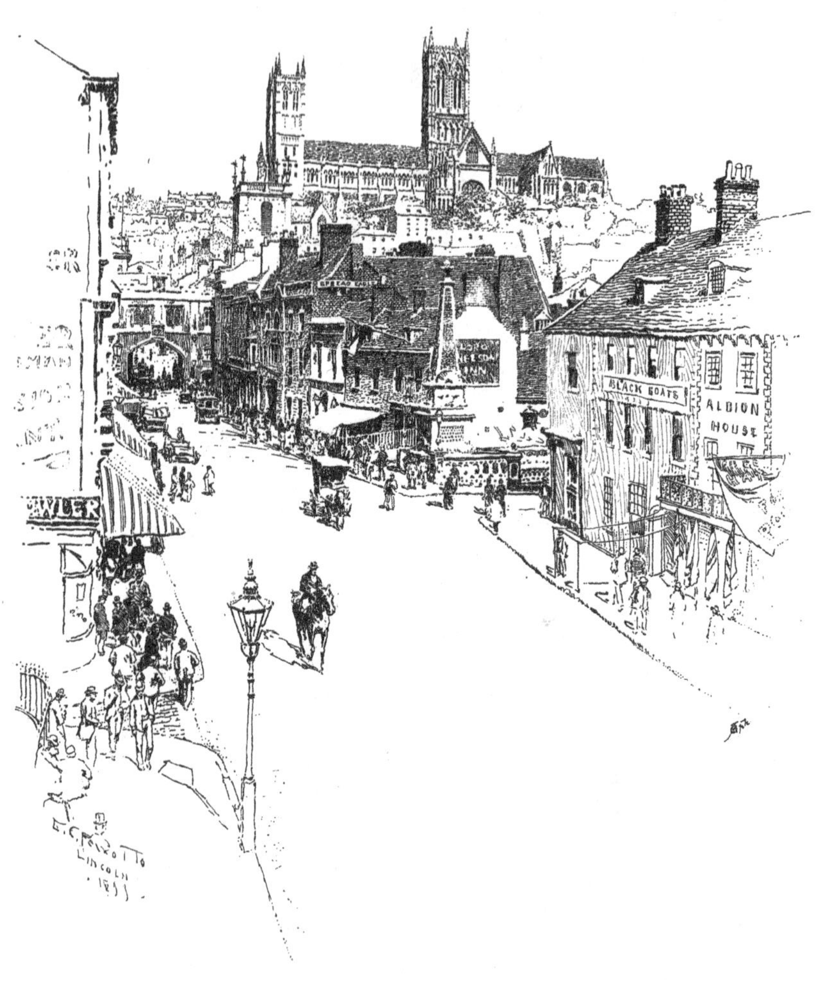

Illustration by Ernest Peixotto, “High Street, Lincoln”

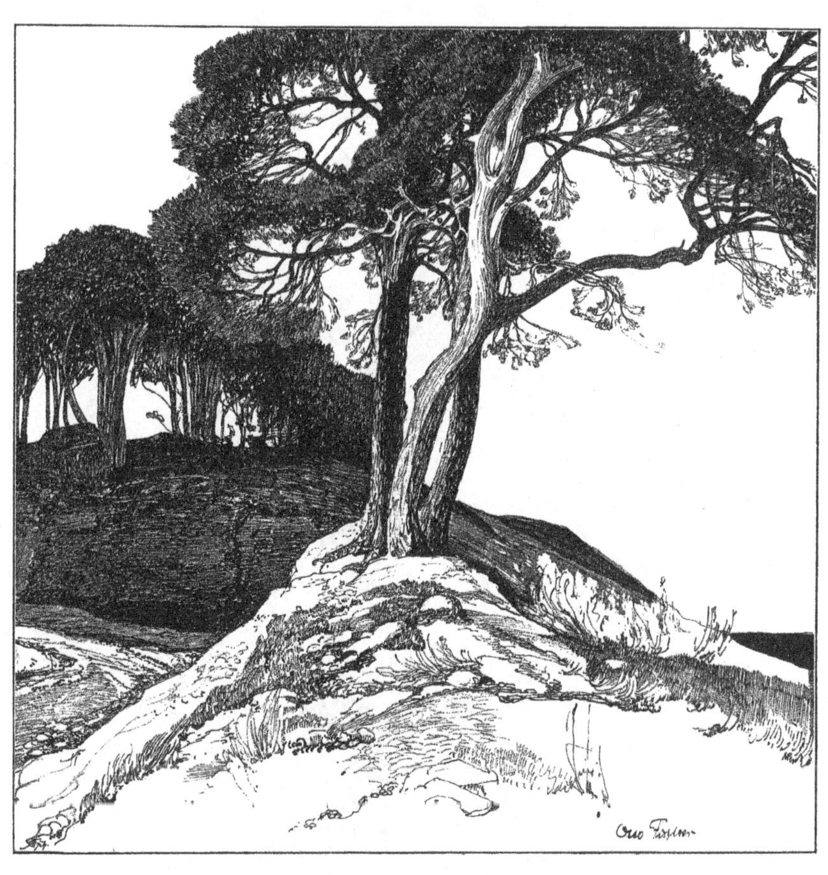

Illustration by Otto Fischer, "A Study"

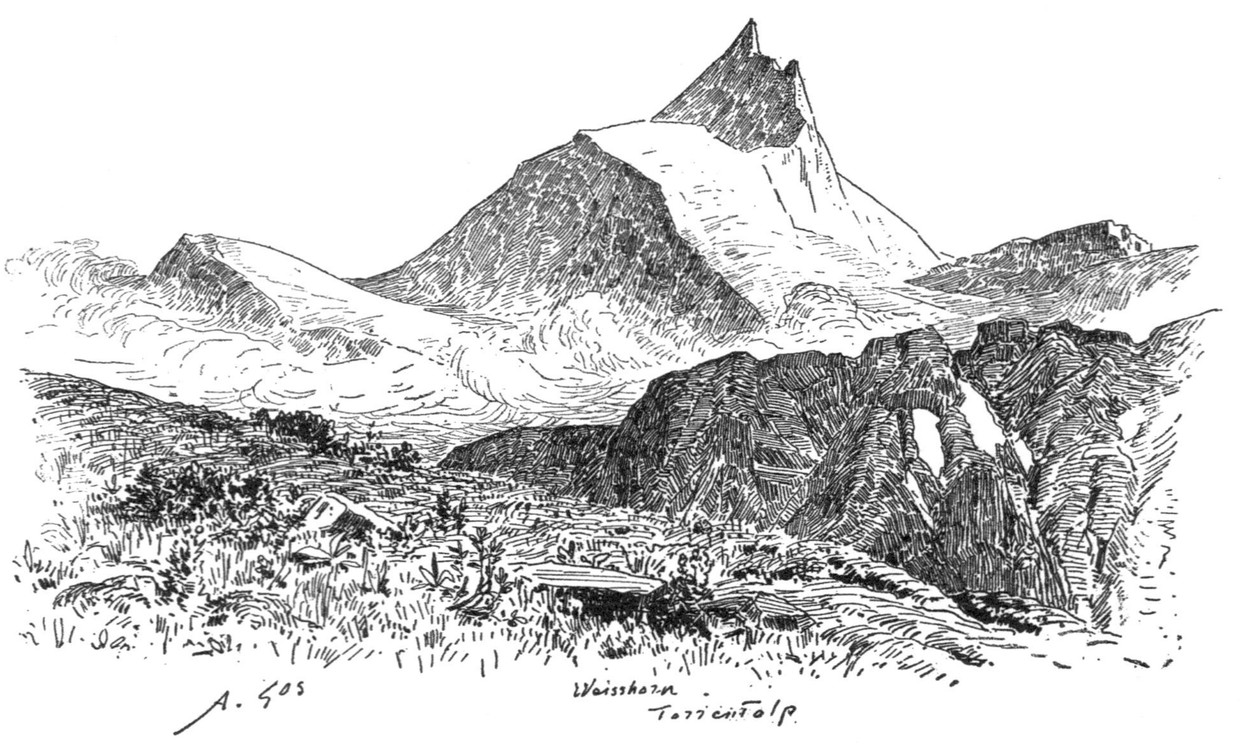

Illustration by Albert Gos, "Weisshorn"

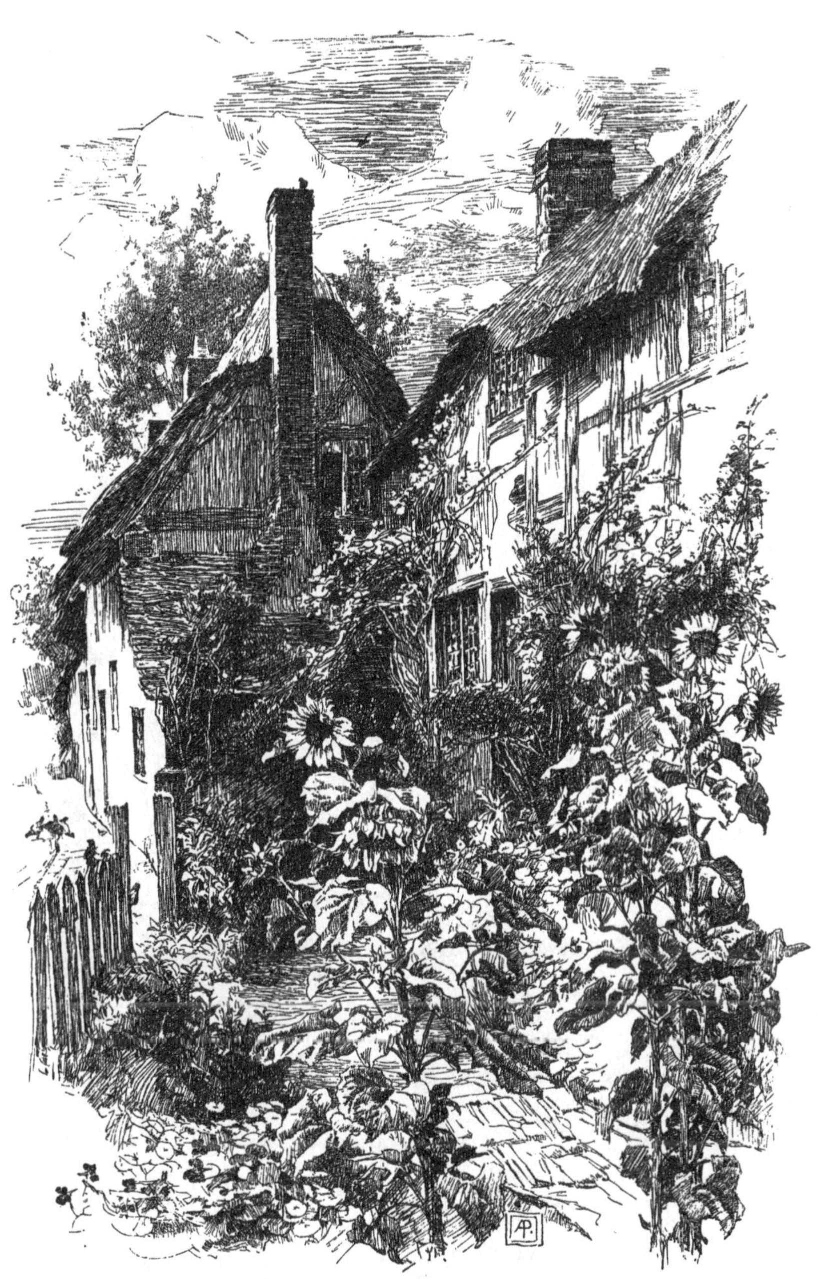

Illustration from *Harper's Magazine*, 1887.

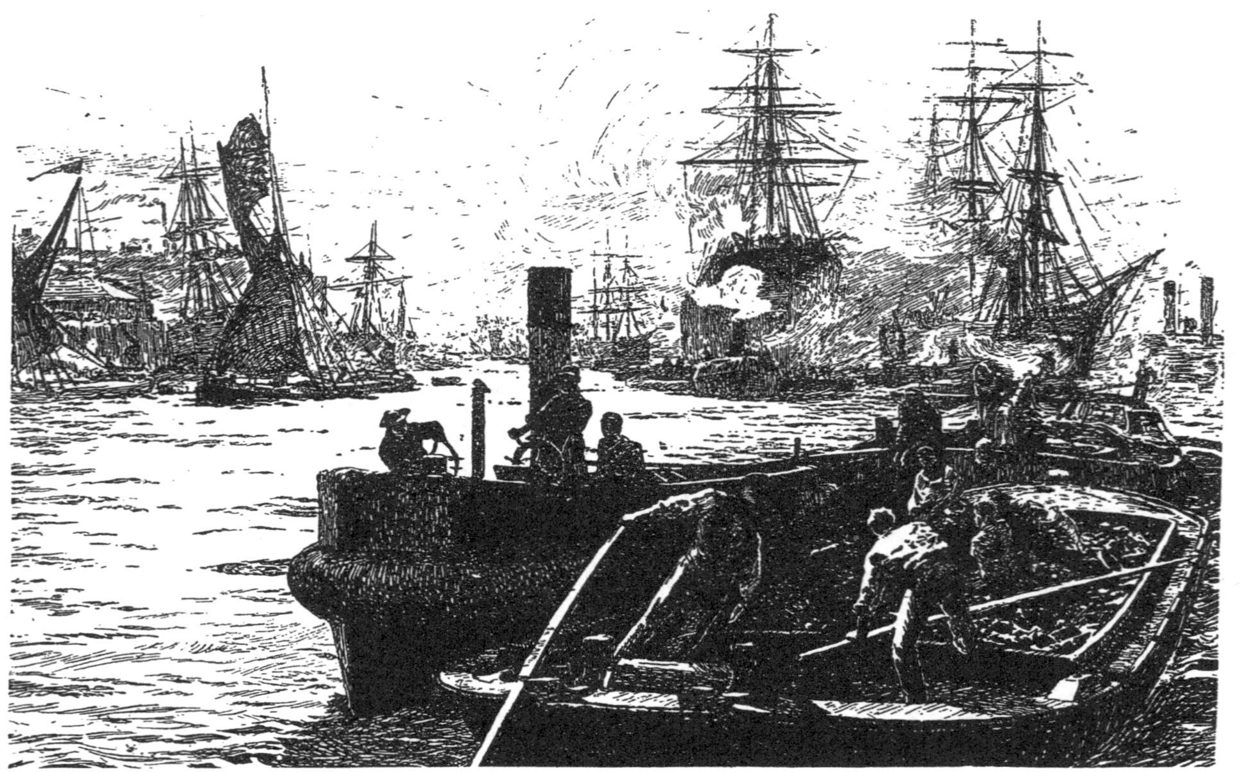

Illustration by W. L. Wyllie, "Toil, Glitter and Grime on the Thames"

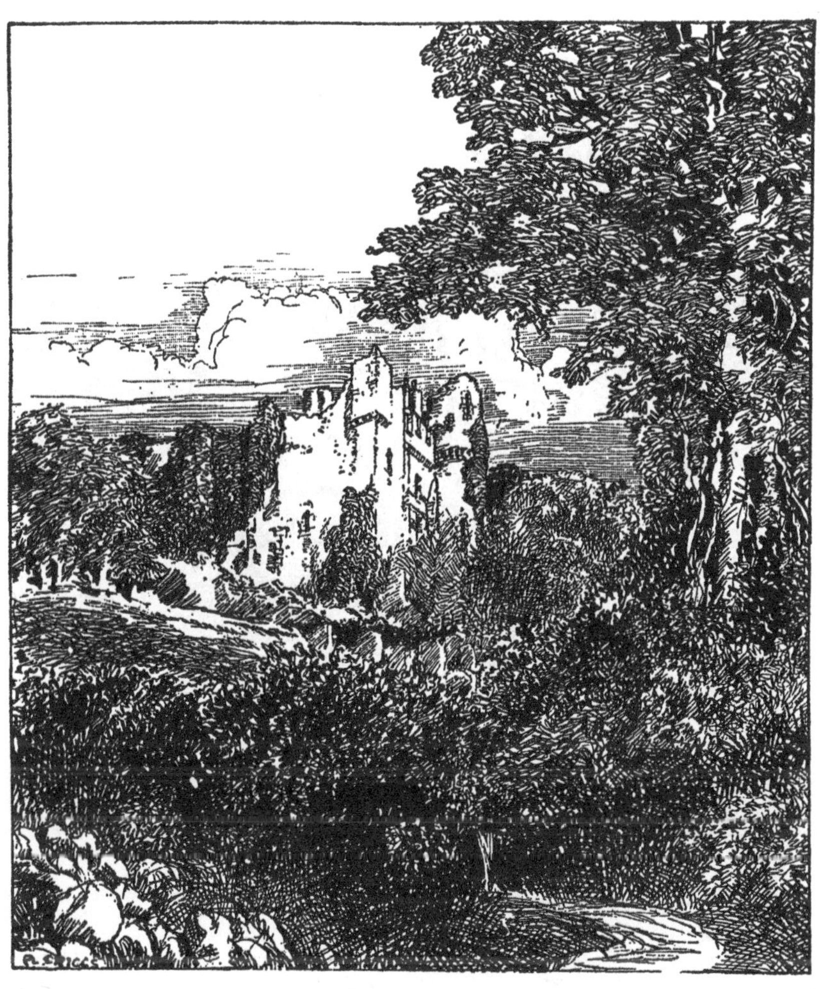

Illustration by F. L. Griggs, “Newport Castle”

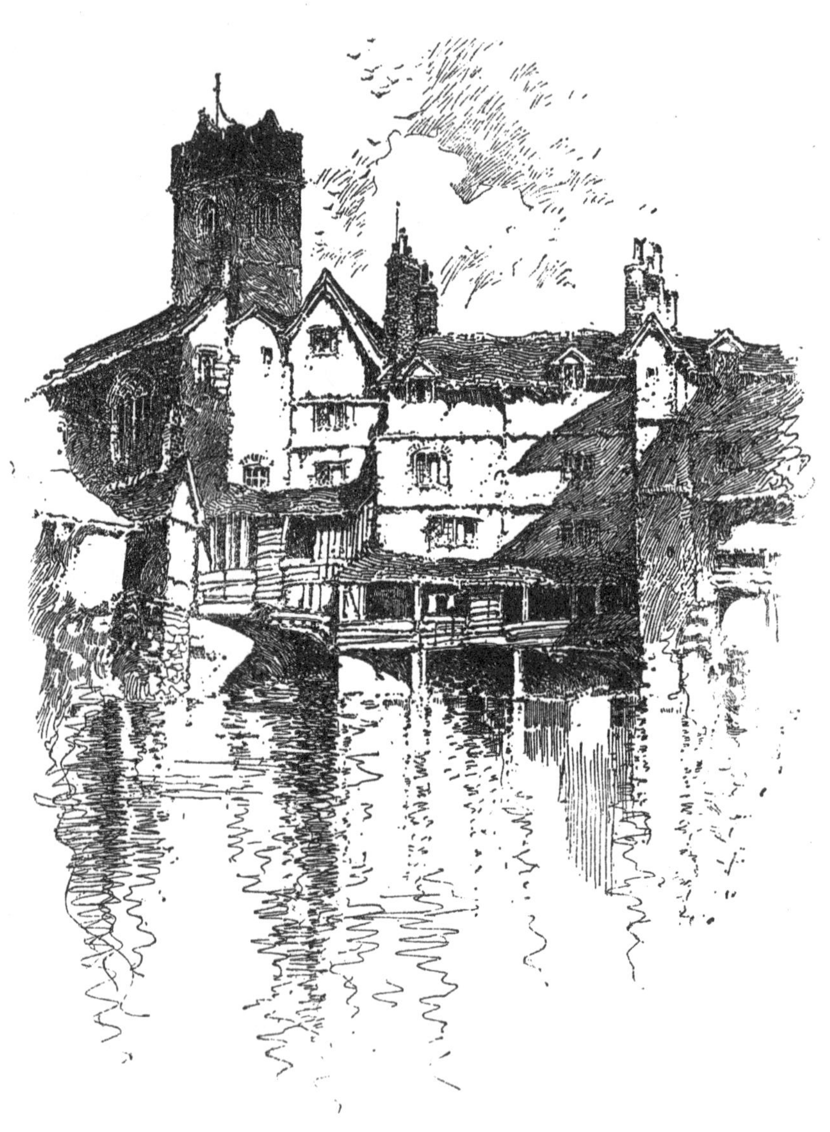

Illustration by Herbert Railton, “Old Houses on Eve Island”

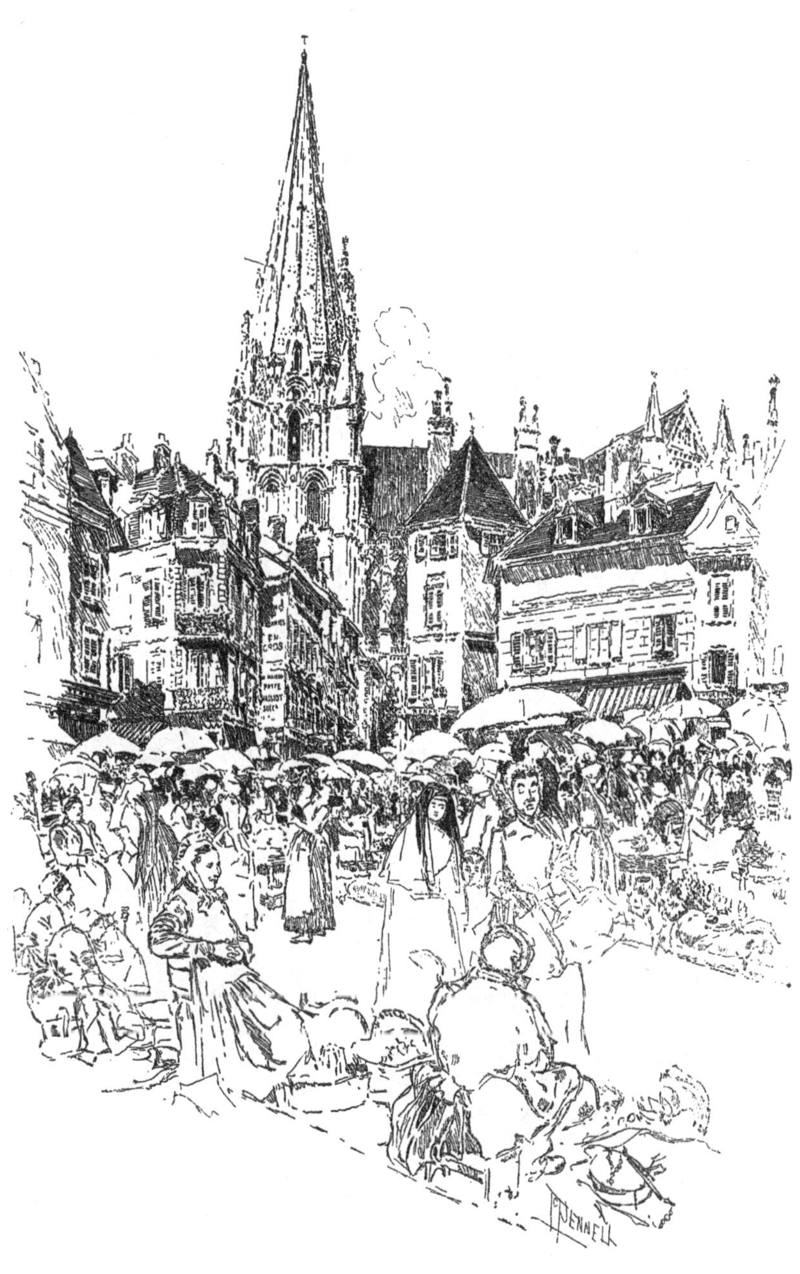

Illustration by Joseph Pennell, “Market Square at Chartres”

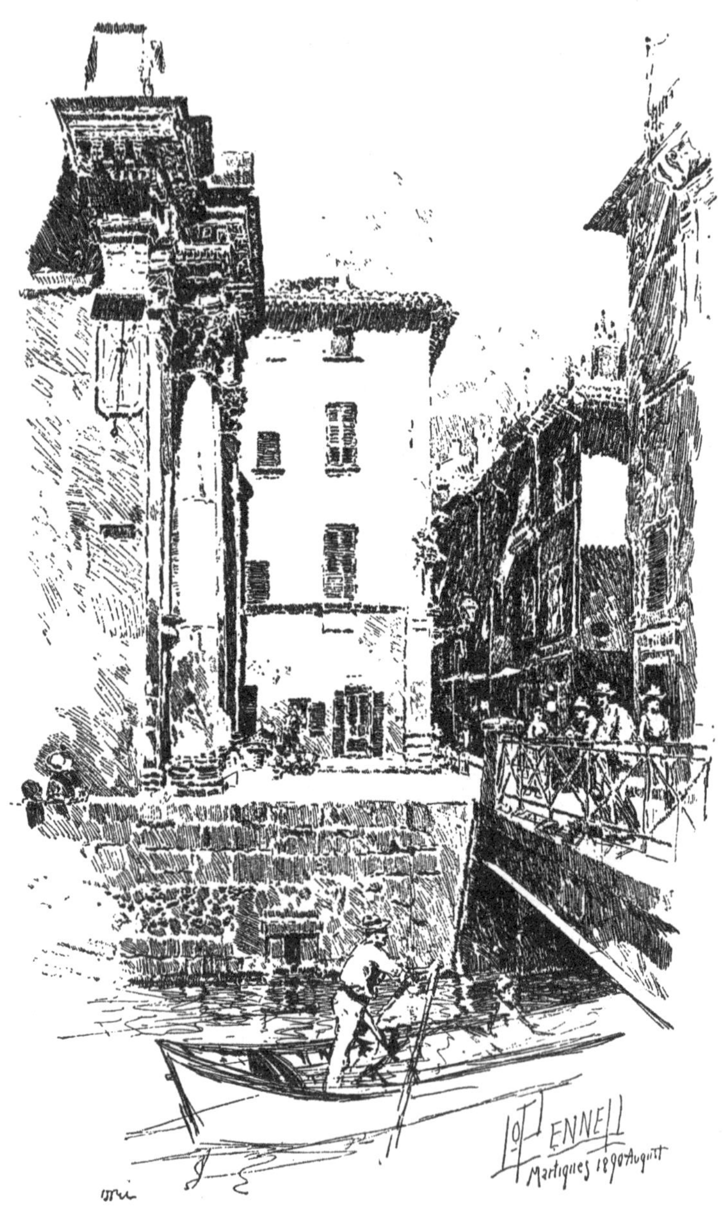

Illustration by Joseph Pennell, "A Street at Martigues"

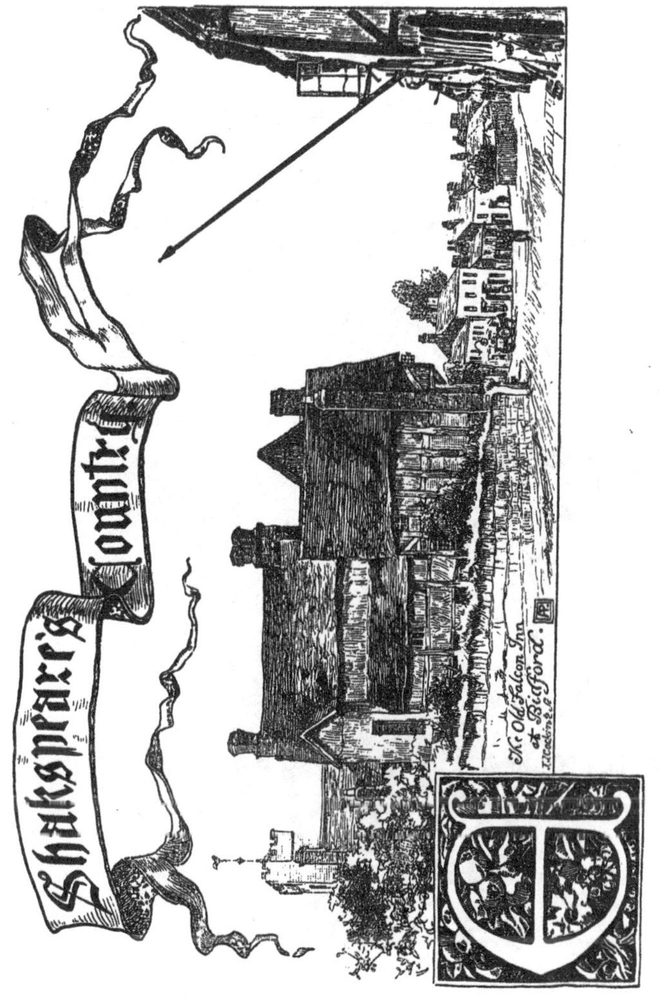

Illustration by Alfred Parsons, "Shakespeare's Country"

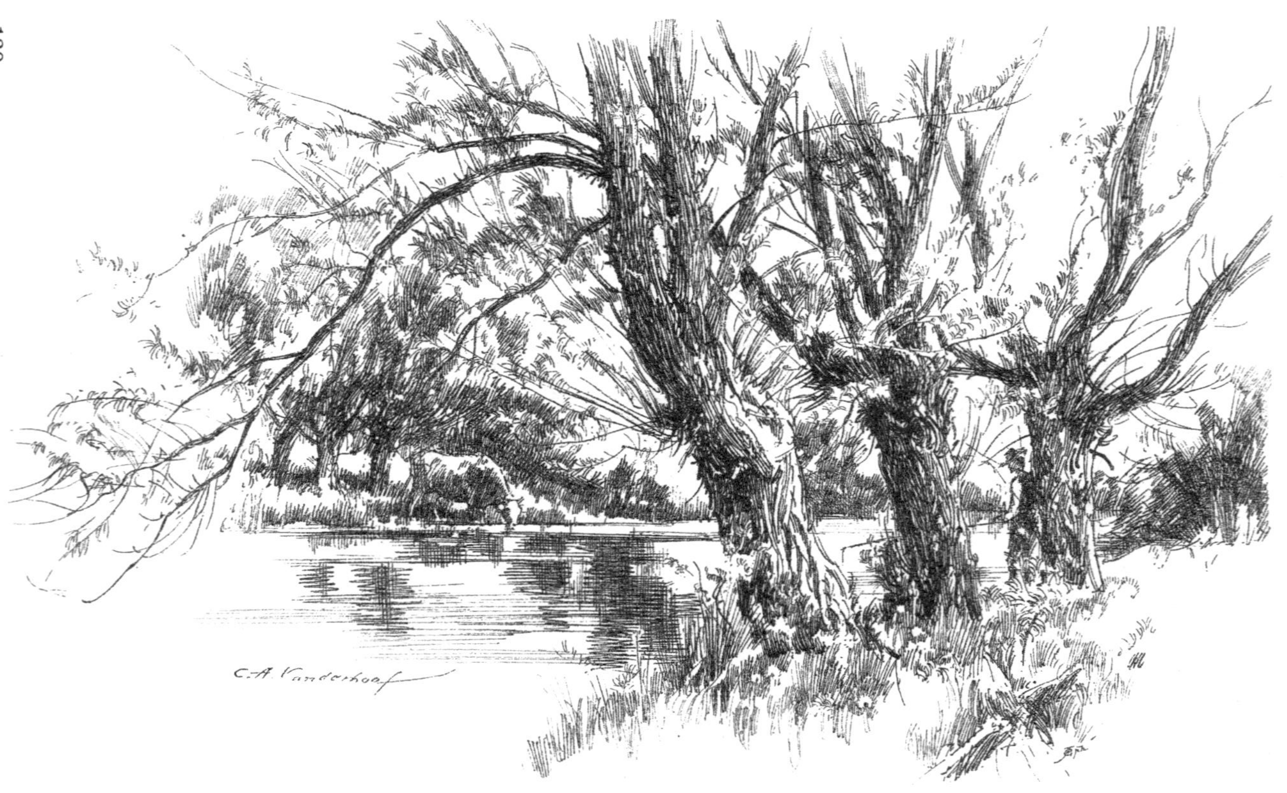

Illustration by Charles A. Vanderhoof, "On the Manasquan River"

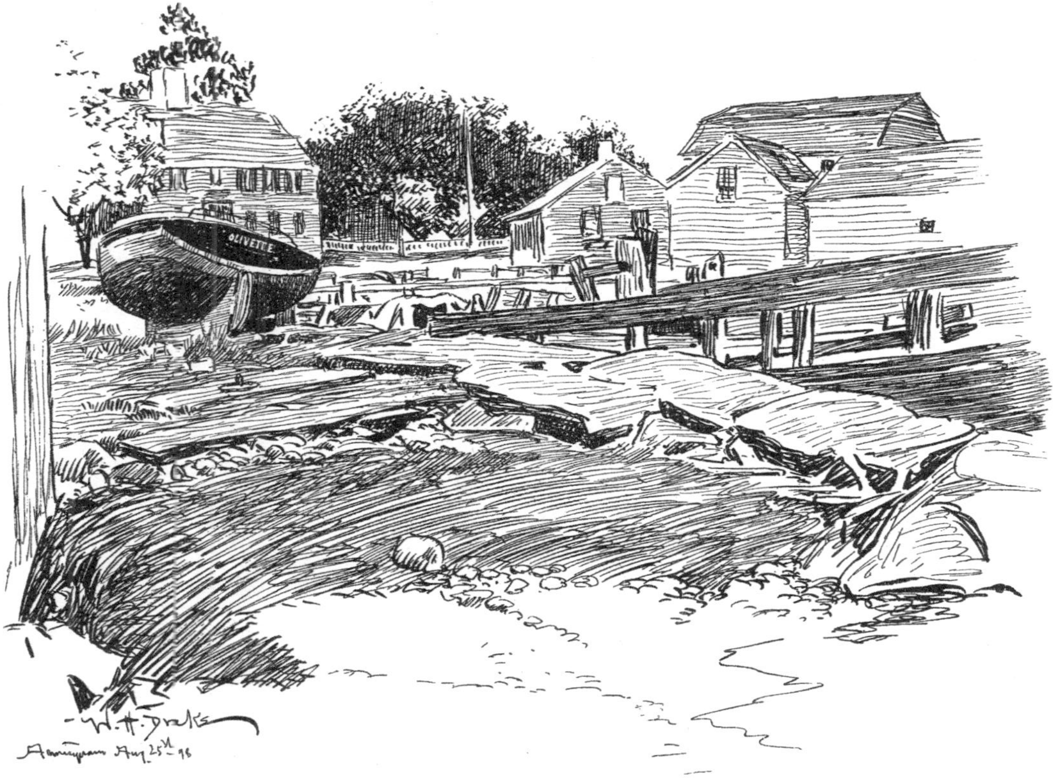

Illustration by W. H. Drake, “A Shipbuilding Yard”